THE MARRIAGE OF MUSHROOMS AND GARLIC

THE Marriage OF Mushrooms AND Garlic

CHESTER AARON *and* MALCOLM CLARK
with Suzanne N. Adams and Surachet Sangsana

PHOTOGRAPHS BY ROGER ADAMS

Zumaya Publications ♦ Austin TX ♦ 2013

THE MARRIAGE OF MUSHROOMS AND GARLIC
© 2013 by Chester Aaron and Malcolm Clark
ISBN 9781612711454
Photographs © Roger Adams
Design © Stephen Tiano

"Zumaya Publications" and the stork logo are trademarks of Zumaya Publications LLC, Austin TX. Look for us online at http://www.zumayapublications.com

Library of Congress Cataloging-in-Publication Data

Aaron, Chester.
  The marriage of mushrooms and garlic / by Chester Aaron and Malcolm Clark ; photographs by Roger Adams ; with Suzanne N. Adams and Surachet Sangsana.
       pages cm.
  Includes bibliographical references and index.
  ISBN 978-1-61271-145-4 (trade pbk. : alk. paper) -- ISBN 978-1-61271-146-1 -- ISBN 978-1-61271-147-8 (epub : alk. paper)
  1. Cooking (Mushrooms) 2. Cooking (Garlic) 3. Mushrooms. 4. Garlic. I. Clark, Malcolm, 1942- II. Title.
  TX804.A215 2013
  641.6'58--dc23
                              2013037967

To my mentor and teacher, the late Dr. Tsuneto Yoshii
—MALCOLM CLARK

Contents

ix

Contents

PHOTO CREDITS

Cover - Roger Adams
First title page - Roger Adams
Pages 1 and 2 (Chester) - Roger Adams
Page 2 (Malcolm) - Surachet Sangsana (Pic)
Page 3 (Malcolm with pom pon) - Gourmet Mushrooms Inc.
Page 4 (pom pon) - Gourmet Mushrooms Inc.
Pages 5 thru 8 - Roger Adams
Page 9 (oyster) - Gourmet Mushrooms Inc.
Pages 10 thru 16 - Roger Adams
Page 17 (shiitake) - Gourmet Mushrooms Inc.
Pages 18 thru 28 - Roger Adams
Page 29 (clamshells) - Gourmet Mushrooms Inc.
Pages 30 thru 45 - Roger Adams
Page 49 (maitaki) - Gourmet Mushrooms Inc.
Pages 50 thru 61 - Roger Adams
Page 62 (basket) - Gourmet Mushrooms Inc.
Page 65 - Roger Adams
Page 70 (bolete) - Gourmet Mushrooms Inc.
Pages 71 and 73 - Roger Adams
Page 75 (chanterelle) - Gourmet Mushrooms Inc.
Pages 76 thru 78 - Roger Adams
Page 79 (morel) - Gourmet Mushrooms Inc.
Pages 80 and 81 - Roger Adams
Page 82 (cordyceps) - Gourmet Mushrooms Inc.
Page 85 (basket) - Gourmet Mushrooms Inc.
Pages 87 and 88 - Roger Adams
Page 90 (Goldy) - Irene Connelly
Page 91 (Goldy) - Irene Connelly
Page 93 (Chester and Goldy) - Serena Enger
Page 99(Malcolm in Thailand) - Surachet Sangsana (Pic)
Page 100 (Chester and owl) - Dyanna Taylor
Page 101 - Roger Adams
Page 102 - Suzanne Adams
Page 103 - Nannette Tiano

Acknowledgments

The advice, photography and friendship of Roger Adams, the culinary talents of chefs Suzanne Adams and Pic (Surachet Sangsana).

Introduction

This is a book about the experiences of Malcolm Clark and Chester Aaron, who, independent of each other, have dedicated a large part of their lives to the development and distribution of unique varieties of mushrooms and garlic for the table as well as for laboratories, benefiting palate as well as body and soul. Their work has had an everlasting influence on food in America.

After much travel to exotic cultures, after years of research, after failures and successes in forests and fields, in kitchens and laboratories, Malcolm and Chester settled in Northern California a few miles from each other among their favorite centuries-old redwoods.

There, they have succeeded in expanding a worldwide appreciation for these various fungi we call mushrooms and this vari-tempered herb we call garlic.

Combining stories about two such different foods is best done by bringing them together in cuisine, where they are magically married. So, this is also a cookbook. The recipes have been prepared by two veteran chefs with years of experience in Eastern and Western cooking.

In cooking, mushrooms often retain their distinctive shape. Texture may change, but generally, their variety can be identified. Garlic, on the other hand, is often cut, chopped or minced, and its visual identity is totally lost in the final presentation.

Not so in this book. Garlic grows in hundreds of varieties, many of them extraordinarily beautiful. The unique photographs of some of the more colorful garlics are scattered throughout these pages and do not remain unnoticed, as they would on the plate.

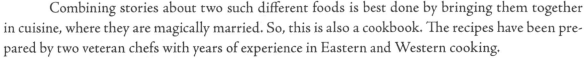

WHY I AM WRITING THIS BOOK
(BY CHESTER)

2

When I met Malcolm Clark twenty years ago, he was the founding president of Gourmet Mushrooms, and he took me on a tour of his laboratory and farm. Subsequent meetings over the years brought to life memories about my father (born in Russia, a farmer in his later life in Pennsylvania). Malcolm took me on journeys to hunt down safely edible wild mushrooms and I soon realized that here, indeed, was a Mushroom God. When he and I decided to write this book, I could only be grateful and confess that I had made a superior, and very beneficial, friend.

WHY I AM WRITING THIS BOOK
(BY MALCOLM)

Often—at a dinner party, hanging out with friends or sitting in an airplane—the subject of mushrooms would come up, and I would find myself telling stories about collecting them, many times in the strangest of places. Getting shot at, for example, along the way down a mountain in Nepal after collecting the elusive medicinal mushroom *Cordyceps*.

One day, at a luncheon attended by chefs and prominent food writers, with Chester talking garlic and I mushrooms, several of the guests present suggested we owed the world a book. So, here you have it—two unusual guys telling their stories and adventures about the *Marriage of Mushrooms and Garlic* and the everlasting influence they have had on cuisine in North America and Europe.

Pom Pon Blanc Mushroom

Pom pon blanc mushroom (AKA bear's tooth, old man's beard, monkey's brain, etc., or by its scientific name *Hericium erinaceous*).

Pom pon blanc was the name I gave it at GMI after I had developed controlled cultivation methods; this was the first time this mushroom had ever been grown commercially. But credit must be shared with the renowned executive chef at Ernie's Restaurant in San Francisco, one of the finest restaurants of its day. When Chef Jacques Rober was first presented with this mushroom to develop some recipes, he said, "Ahh, *oui!* This must be pom pon blanc."

And so it was named, and as the first-time cultivators we claimed the right to name it. After all, you could not present it in a dish named, say, Dover sole marinara and old man's beard or Dover sole marinara and monkey's brain. That would certainly not sell. But sole marinara accompanied by pom pon blanc mushrooms sounds good and tastes delicious.

TAMING THE SHROOM

No mushroom is closer to my heart than this, the pom pon blanc. Being credited as the first person in the world to cultivate this exotic fungus, I feel like its proud parent.

This is the short story of its birth.

In 1983, on a normal workday at GMI, a local mushroom aficionado brought in a beautiful mushroom for identification. I immediately recognized it as *Hericium erinaceous*, one of the so-called toothed fungi that really do not look like mushrooms at all, having no typical stem or cap. Instead, it's round, white, and covered with downward-pointing soft spines; it's often the size of a tennis ball but can grow to football size.

5

Having tasted this quite rare mushroom before, I became obsessed with the idea of growing it. I needed a fresh specimen so I could harvest either spores or a tissue culture. The gentleman who brought the mushroom in for identification kindly gave me its approximate location which was not too far away near a town called Glen Ellen in eastern Sonoma County, California.

I took the short drive over to the area in hopes of finding more mushrooms, and sure enough, there they were, growing on the side of a recently fallen oak tree. I rushed home, gathered up some instruments so I could tune into its growing habitat. I needed a light meter, a temperature/humidity probe, and a sleeping bag, as I intended to live with this mushroom so I could get to know it better. After all, I was going to have to duplicate its happy home if I ever hoped to grow it.

A few days later, I was back in the lab, having successfully taken a tissue culture, and the mycelium was growing happily on a sterilized Petri dish. This could be referred to as the pregnancy; the birth was several months away.

Finally, on some repaired-wood-chip growing media containers and in a controlled environment similar to the place I had found them, small round white mushrooms appeared and, over the next few days, matured into golf- to tennis ball-sized specimens. The pom pon blanc was born.

MEDICINAL VALUES

Apparently, some Native Americans would carry dried, powdered *Hericium* mushrooms in their medicine bags, and if they had a bleeding injury, they would sprinkle it on the wound to stop the bleeding. So it must have a styptic effect, which is supported by the fact the Chinese in recent years developed a pill used to treat stomach ailments, including bleeding ulcers. Other, more recent research indicates that *Hericium* is effective in treating several other medical conditions.

Pom Pon Blanc Mushroom

Pom Pon Recipes

POM PON MUSHROOM IN PASTA

8 ounces fresh pom pon mushrooms

When making pasta dishes such as a creamy alfredo, try taking a pom pon mushroom and tearing off thin strips. It will almost look like crabmeat. Then, when your pasta dish is cooked and ready, mix in the strips of mushrooms and serve. They will even have a hint of crab flavor.

POM-PON MUSHROOM TEMPURA

8 ounces fresh pom pon blanc mushrooms
³/₄ C. sifted plain (all purpose) flour
1 C. ice-cold water
1 large egg, beaten
2–3 ice cubes
1 C. cooking oil

Slice mushrooms into 1-inch pieces.

To make the batter, pour the ice-cold water into a mixing bowl, add the beaten egg and mix well. Add the flour and very lightly fold in with a pair of chopsticks or a fork. *Do not beat.* The batter should still be quite lumpy. Add the ice cubes.

Heat cooking oil until the temperature reaches about 300° F—it will sizzle when you drip a bit of batter mix into it.

Gently coat the slices of mushrooms in the batter one at a time and place them into the hot oil. Remove when lightly browned and drain on a paper towel. They are now ready to eat.

Serve with other tempura ingredients such as prawns, sliced fish, shiitake mushrooms, vegetables.

The Marriage of Mushrooms & Garlic

Oyster Mushroom

Also known by its scientific name *Plurotus* and in this case *Plurotus ostreatus*. It is generally found on dead or dying trees and stumps. There are dozens of variants of this bordering on pretty mushroom with colors ranging from white, cream and brown to gun-metal blue, yellow, and pink. And then there's my oyster mushroom: the *baby blue oyster*.

It was baptized this by some friends and myself; I refer to them as my naming committee. We cook up a batch of a mushroom in various ways, and then, armed with an appropriate bottle

of wine, we feast and discuss what it should be called. I don't always get my way, but in this case I did. We called it the baby blue oyster because it was small (no more than an inch across) and reminded one of my friends of the name given Frank Sinatra (Old Blue Eyes). Anyway, this is the name that stuck and has been marketed successfully for years and years.

Like the pom pon blanc, this mushroom also has a special place in my heart.

I was on a trip to Indonesia, and while driving around, I stopped at a small market a few miles up the road from the town of Ubud on the island of Bali. The shapes, colors, and smells were something to behold. Fruits, vegetables, roots and spices of all shapes and sizes, and there, next to some exotic red fruit, was a cluster of blue oyster mushrooms. That was it, I had to know more and, if possible, go to the place they

had been found and collect some specimens. I was able to find someone to do the translating for me, and arrangements were made for me to meet up with the person who had collected the mushrooms.

At first light the following morning, I woke up and soon was traveling up the hill to meet my guide-to-be. When I reached the market, which was not yet set up, there was my man, waiting anxiously to take me into the forest to find the mushrooms.

It was about an hour's walk up a damp, misty path, constantly looking out for snakes and biting insects. Finally, we reached our destination, and all over the base of an old tree were bunches of this beautiful mushroom.

I grabbed my camera, took some shots and made a few notes in my notebook, gathered up a bunch of nice, fresh young specimens and headed back down the path to the market. After reaching the market and my car, I started to change my soaking wet shirt and was horrified to find that several small leeches had worked their way under my clothing and clung to my skin. It took almost an hour using salt and toothpicks to get the stubborn little creatures off.

Despite the discomfort, it was okay—I had my mushrooms.

Back at the hotel, I got out my little agar test tubes (never leave home without them) and created a mini-lab environment. With a razor blade, I dissected out small sections of mushroom, lit an alcohol-soaked cotton ball and carefully passed them through the flame. I then placed them into the test tubes and closed them up tightly. The tissue culture collection was complete.

I finished the remainder of my trip photographing and collecting orchids (my second passion).

By the time I returned to the states and was back in the lab, the insides of the agar tubes were covered with mycelium, and I had what I needed to create spawn and seed out some growing material. About four weeks later, lots of little oyster mushrooms covered the growth material (mainly wood chips).

They turned out to be fairly easy to grow, and we had now added a new mushroom to our fungus bank.

RECIPES

Mushroom-and-Garlic Chowder and Oyster Mushroom Fritters.

MEDICINAL VALUES

The oyster mushroom (*Pleurotus ostreatus*) contains a substance called mevinolin that can be effective in lowering high cholesterol. It also contains many beneficial active enzymes.

The Marriage of Mushrooms & Garlic

Oyster Mushroom Recipes

MUSHROOM AND GARLIC CHOWDER

^{1}/$_4$ pound of bacon
2 C. sliced celery
1 onion, chopped
8 ounces of oyster mushrooms
^{1}/$_4$ C. flour
1 C. chicken or vegetable broth
1 C. cream
^{1}/$_2$ C. milk
4 cloves of minced garlic
salt and white pepper to taste

Cut the bacon into ^{1}/$_2$ inch slices. Sauté until crisp. Set aside. Reserve 2 tbsp. bacon fat. Place the bacon fat in a medium-sized heavy-bottomed saucepan. Add the celery, onion and mushrooms. Cook on medium heat while stirring until done. Sprinkle with the flour and stir to combine well. Add the broth and cook until thickened. Add the cream and enough of the milk to obtain a consistency to your liking. Add the garlic and salt and pepper to taste. Spoon into soup bowls and garnish with the crispy bacon bits.

OYSTER MUSHROOM FRITTERS

8 ounces fresh medium-sized oyster mushrooms
2 egg whites
½ C. all-purpose flour
Cooking oil

For the dipping sauce
2 tbsp. fish sauce
2 tbsp. lime juice
1 clove of garlic, minced
Pinch of dry chili flakes

Separate the oyster mushrooms to bite-size. If you need to clean them, use a brush and do not wash. Heat cooking oil until the temperature reaches about 300° F.

Deep-fry the mushroom.

Dip each mushroom in egg white and dust in the flour. Gently slip it into the oil and cook until it goes crisp then turn over to the other side. Drain on kitchen paper.

Arrange the mushrooms on a plate. Serve immediately with a dipping sauce of your choice.

How This All Began
by Chester Aaron

I grew up in a coal-mining village in western Pennsylvania during the Great Depression. My father, an emigre from Russia, owned the only store in the village; and although the shelves were often empty, the produce boxes were usually filled with fruits and vegetables and herbs from our garden.

The plant in that garden most treasured by both my mother and father: garlic.

My mother, a slight and beautiful and deceptively delicate emigre from Poland (they met on the boat) accompanied the sopranos who sang opera every Saturday on our large Philco radio (Station KDKA, Pittsburgh). When she was not cooking or cleaning or listening to opera, she was

crocheting elaborate edgings for pillow slips or doilies, works of art that won prizes every summer at the Butler County Fair.

My father, when he was not lamenting the lack of income to fill the shelves of the store and guarantee additional income, was in the field behind our house, planting or harvesting.

My brothers, as they grew up, were never interested in the garden. They either were in college or working in the steel mills in town, three miles to the south of our village. I, as I grew up, leaped at every opportunity to work in the field at my father's side. His and my favorite food to plant and nourish and harvest and eat: garlic.

But garlic was not there just to be eaten.

When I or anyone in the family suffered bruises or cuts or had to fight off colds or other mysterious ailments, my mother, as well as my father, relied on garlic.

The Marriage of Mushrooms & Garlic

My father: *"Idi! Vozmi mne chesnok!"* "Go! Get me the garlic!"

If and when one of my brothers or my mother or I had an earache, we bent or leaned into the position that would best permit my father to squeeze a peeled and crushed garlic clove into the target ear.

We needed no medical ointment in the house. Whenever we cut or bruised ourselves, a peeled clove, cut in half to expose two moist surfaces, would be rubbed on the injury, twice, three, four times a day, for a day, for two days, for three days. The pain would flee immediately, and recovery would continue forever.

"I got piles," my father announced one evening at the supper table. "Chester! *Idi! Vozmi mne chesnok!*"

In Pennsylvania English: "Chester! Go! Get me the garlic."

Piles: the local term for hemorrhoids.

I went to the kitchen cupboard where, in three or four bags, my mother and father stored that year's harvest. Available: three or four or five varieties, bulbs with skins white to pink to red; bulbs with four or five large cloves or ten or twelve smaller ones.

"The red," my father called. "Bring the red."

I selected the bag with the bulbs encased in the red skins, removed one bulb, took it to my father. Using his thumbnail, Pappa dug free two cloves from the collection of eight or ten red-skinned bodies. He bit off the tip of one clove, used his fingernails to remove the skin, rolled the clove in his fingers to soften the interior.

How This All Began

16

Taking a large swallow of his hot black Swee-Touch-nee tea, he stood at the side of the supper table and unbuckled his belt. After his trousers dropped, he shimmied his shorts to the floor, bent over, shoved the entire clove inside his ass as far up as he could shove it.

"Oy," he said. "It burns. It works."

Taking no chances, he processed a second clove and, bent over again, inserted same.

After four or five minutes, as the silence continued, Poppa reached to the table, lifted his cup, swallowed another gulp of his black tea. Then he straightened, pulled up his shorts, pulled up his pants, buckled his belt.

"Done," he said. *"Est besser und besser."*

I remember my mother performing the same ritual twice, but each time she required privacy. She processed the treatment in the room in which she and my father slept.

Many years later, in combat in Germany, I was more than once reminded of my mother and father's love of garlic for the treatment of pain and/or cut or bruise.

Russian soldiers did not have penicillin in their medical kits.

How many times … ten? twenty? … did I see a wounded Russian soldier, pants down or sleeves up, wounds on arms or legs or bodies bleeding, reach into a pocket and remove a clove or two of garlic and use his teeth to peel the clove and apply the moist surface and rub and rub.

I could hear my father's voice, always, each time: *"Est besser und besser."*

Now, almost seventy years since that war and those memories, I lift one of my so-called garlic books or I look at my beautiful garlic poster. (Thank you, Ten Speed Press; thank you, Random House!) I see my mother's angelic smile as she accepts another award for her art, I hear my father's *"Est besser und besser … ."*

The Marriage of Mushrooms & Garlic

Shiitake Mushroom

AKA Chinese black mushroom, dong-goo, Black Forest mushroom and by its scientific name, *Lentinula edodes.* The list goes on and on, but probably the most accepted name here in North America and Europe is shiitake, and that certainly applies to Japan, as this is a Japanese word. The shii is a type of oak, and the name basically means "the mushroom of the shii tree."

This is one of the most popular mushrooms in the world and has a long history in Asian cuisine, going back more than a thousand years. Today, it is no longer the sacred possession of Asia and is now cultivated around the world, thanks in part to the generous sharing of technology by my mentor and teacher, Dr. Tsuneto Yoshii.

This mushroom, known as hodagi, normally took two years to grow and had been cultivated for decades on hardwood logs about a meter long. It was becoming obvious to Dr. Yoshii that the demand for such valuable hardwood was going to create a serious probem, and shortages were already apparent.

So, seeking a solution to the problem, he devised a method whereby the mushrooms could be grown on wood chips and sawdust, by-products of sawmills and other wood-processing operations.

The problem was solved—well, at least for several more decades.

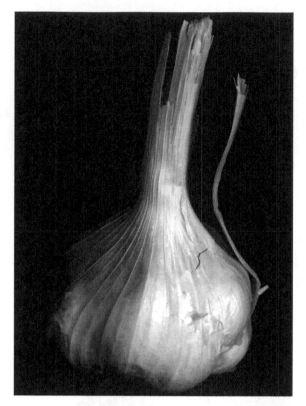

He cleverly formulated a mix of fine wood chips, rice bran, and water, placed it in containers that were then steam-sterilized (like in a pressure cooker) and allowed to cool, and then inoculated (seeded it) with mushroom spawn, which then grew and spread in these plastic containers. Several months later, delectable little shiitake mushrooms would start to grow on the surface of the wood-chip mix. This became known as the Yoshii method.

Regrettably, very few people are aware of this information, even though these were the humble beginnings of what has now become a worldwide, multi-billion-dollar agritech business.

My role in this, as Dr. Yoshii's only non-Japanese student, was to bring this technology out of Japan, change and adapt it to its new environments so that people of other countries could enjoy this incredibly delicious and versatile mushroom, prized not just for its culinary uses but also for its nutritional and medicinal values.*

The vehicle for this work was a company formed in 1970 by a dedicated group of Japanese-Canadians called Shiitake of Canada Ltd. The group (all part-timers), led by dear friend Sam Baba, took over an old button mushroom farm in New Market, a town just north of Toronto. Utilizing Dr. Yoshii's basic technology, we improvised and developed a version of his method suitable for its new environment. It took a few years, but after many hits and misses, we eventually developed the first controlled cultivation process for the shiitake mushroom and introduced them to the waiting marketplace. This was to become a milestone in the mushroom industry and agriculture as a whole.

The demand, while it increased gradually, was certainly there; and many of the Asian customers were quite knowledgeable. They had used it for years in its dry form and also knew about its versatile uses and its health attributes. Now it was available fresh, and that made a big difference.

A few years later, in 1977 and after many difficult decisions involving friends, my occupation and my love of Canada, I sold my home in Toronto, moved to the United States, and trans-

*It was the potential medicinal use of shiitakes that first aroused my interest in fungi, and the research work of Dr. Yoshii that eventually caused me to take a completely different direction in my life.

The Marriage of Mushrooms & Garlic

ferred this technology to the northern California town of Sebastopol. With the blessings of the original group at Shiitake of Canada ltd. I organized a new group and, with principal partners David Law and his brother Philip, we formed a new company called Gourmet Mushrooms Inc. Soon, we had land, buildings and employees to really launch the shiitake mushroom.

From these early beginnings, the shiitake's popularity and the demand for it grew all over North America, spreading into Europe and beyond, seeding the growth of even more new companies.

Sadly, many of these companies are now gone. Even Gourmet Mushrooms no longer cultivates shiitake. This is due to the massive production of this mushroom in China.

The Chinese, using the basic technology developed by Dr. Yoshii, have developed new growing methods. This, combined with the utilization of other growing materials to produce shiitakes on a massive scale with inexpensive labor, overwhelmed the majority of North American growers. Many went out of business.

Fortunately, some survived. Using certified organic growing methods, they grew for a niche market that has expanded. Now, more than a decade later, North American-grown shiitake are making a well-deserved comeback. Because it is nearly impossible for China to meet the strict organic protocol, the future looks good again for the North American grower. (Buy locally grown.)

There is so much more that could be told about my romance with this mushroom. The pom pon blanc made me feel like a proud parent, but the shiitake makes me feel like its romantic lover.

RECIPES

There are thousands of recipes for the shiitake, mostly Asian, but it's been well adapted into Western cuisine, as many already know. Many folks today are using woks to cook with, so try some sliced vegetables, sliced or diced meat, (chicken is good), slices of shiitake mushrooms, a crushed garlic clove and a little added flavoring (oyster or soy sauce) stir-fried in the wok hot and fast. The family will love it.

MEDICINAL VALUES

The shiitake mushroom (*Lentinula edodes*) has a long history not only for its culinary uses but also for its nutritional and medicinal values—it is truly a functional food. However, its most impressive achievement is its use in an FDA-approved drug known as Lentinan. Used in the treatment of cancer, it is reputed to be a non-invasive adjunct to chemotherapy.

It has extensive use in modern applications of Traditional Chinese Medicine.

Shiitake Mushroom

Shiitake Mushroom Recipes

WINE COUNTRY SHIITAKE FRITTATA

Wonderful served with eggs at breakfast, or as finger food snacks.

1 medium onion, diced
1 clove garlic, minced
8 oz. fresh shiitake mushrooms, finely diced
3 tbsp. olive oil
6 eggs, beaten

$^1/_4$ C. bread crumbs
$^1/_2$ tsp. salt
$^1/_8$ tsp. each oregano, white pepper, Tabasco
$^1/_2$ pound Monterey Jack cheese, grated
2 tbsp. finely chopped fresh cilantro

Preheat oven to 325° F

Saute onions, garlic, and shiitake in olive oil over medium heat until slightly limp; add to beaten eggs. Combine with all remaining ingredients, mixing well.

Turn into a buttered pan 7 x 11-inch pan. Bake for approximately 30 minutes, or until lightly browned.

Remove, let cool, cut into bite-size squares and serve.

GARLIC PORK WITH SHIITAKE MUSHROOM (MOO GRATIEM)

The blend of garlic and pepper makes this a simple and tasty dish to make.

2 pounds sliced pork loin
1 pound cut or whole (if size is small) shiitake mushrooms

1 tbsp. fish sauce
2 tbsp. Thai soy sauce or maggi sauce
2 tbsp. chopped fresh garlic
$^{1}/_{2}$ tbsp. white ground pepper
$^{1}/_{2}$ tbsp. black ground pepper
2 tbsp. of oyster sauce
$^{1}/_{2}$ c cooking oil
1 tbsp. chopped fresh cilantro

21

Heat the skillet and cook garlic with oil on medium heat. Stir in the pork and mushrooms, cook for 5 minutes or until the pork is cooked through. Add fish sauce, Thai soy sauce, oyster sauce, white pepper and black pepper. Stir well to combine all ingredients.

Serve on a plate and garnish with fresh cilantro.

Shiitake Mushroom Recipes

22

CREAM OF MUSHROOM AND GARLIC SOUP

1 pound shiitake mushrooms
4 tbsp. butter
1 onion, chopped
1/4 c flour
2 c of chicken or vegetable stock
2 c half & half
4 ounces of goat cheese
4 garlic cloves, minced
salt and white pepper to taste
4 tbsp. of cream sherry

Separate the mushroom caps from the stalks. Chop the stalks and thinly slice the mushrooms. In a heavy-bottomed sauté pan, melt the butter. Add the onions and mushrooms. Cook on medium heat until soft and cooked through. Remove a few of the sliced mushroom caps and set aside. Sprinkle the remaining mushrooms with the flour and stir to combine. Add the stock and cook until thickened. Add the half & half. Stir in the minced garlic. Cool slightly then pour into a food processor and process until smooth. Return to the saucepan and heat. Add the goat cheese and stir until cheese is completely melted. Add salt and pepper to taste. Add the cream sherry. Stir to com-bine. Pour into individual serving bowls and garnish with reserved mushroom cap slices. Serve immediately.

The Marriage of Mushrooms & Garlic

The Tasting (Yuck!)

The night I received Earl Gladiola's message, I typed it out on my computer and printed it and saved it and here it is: "Hi, Chester, this is Earl. Be sure to reserve the evening of the 20th for a world-shakey wine tasting. Place: Our own li'l ol' Gladiola Winery. Wear clothes. There will be 3 rich world-famous wine-makers, 4 rich world-famous wine-writers. Only peasants at the table: my wife, my daughter, you, me."

How had the small insignificant owner of the small insignificant Gladiola Winery in Sonoma County in California earned such an honor?

Answer: l-u-c-k.

Earl, at the urging of his wife Amalia and his daughter Thalia, had purchased a ticket in an international lottery sponsored by the American Academy of Wineries (offices in Paris and New York City, of course). Cost of one ticket: $1,000. Number of tickets purchased (in Europe, Asia, the U.S.): 898.

Earl's ticket won first prize: a wine-tasting at the winning winemaker's winery with coverage by PBS and NPR and CNN.

Earl Gladiola and his wife Amalia (and daughter Thalia) grow the same variety of grape (Alicante Bouschet) their parents and grandparents grew on the same hundred acres that comprise Gladiola Winery.

Earl: "I love our wine Natalia's Ottimo. My mother Natalia made that wine from these grapes. I love our wine Matthew's Bellezza because my father Matthew made that wine from these grapes. In truth, to me, both wines taste the same. Amalia and Thalia say they can usually taste a difference. Usually, not always."

Amalia: "We are grateful to Safeways all over the country for selling both wines ..."

Thalia: "And to Costcos all over the country for selling both wines. Does Costco or Safeway sell your garlic, Chester?"

Chester: "No."

I met the Gladiolas about ten years ago. Thalia, then in high school, had read one of my young-adult novels and convinced her teacher to invite me to her class. When she learned that I was also a garlic farmer, with three non-fiction books published about that career, and lived less than twenty miles from Gladiola Winery, she told her parents about me, and the very next day they invited me to their home, meaning Gladiola Winery.

Thalia pleaded with me to bring copies of my garlic books to show her parents.

"They won't read your novels, Chester, unless they're on Netflix."

I brought, as gifts, copies of all three garlic books, along with the big beautiful poster my publisher had just put on the market. (Note: it is now out of print.) The poster contains, against a mat-black background, gorgeous photographs (thank you, Susanne Kaspar) of the 45 different varieties of garlic I was then growing and selling all over the world. (Another note: much much older now, finding it harder to push a wheelbarrow or lift a shovel full of moist soil, I am currently growing 21 varieties.)

All three Gladiolas pleaded with me to sell them two or three varieties they could plant in the large fenced garden at the rear of their home.

"I use garlic," Earl said, "on everything, including my toilet paper."

Amalia punched Earl from the left, Thalia punched him from the right.

"I will never sell my garlics to you," I declared. "But I will give them to you. How about ten varieties to plant the first year? Next year, you decide which varieties, if any, you like the best and then just plant and grow those varieties. The way you've done with your grapes."

"I'm glad," Amalia said, "I thought of that."

Over a period of about two weeks, working in the yard behind their home, I constructed three boxes using lumber from one of the redwoods that had fallen many years ago on my own four acres. Each box would hold the more than 350–400 cloves I intended to plant for the Gladiolas.

The Marriage of Mushrooms & Garlic

When planting time (September) arrived, the three Gladiolas worked with me so the next year they could do it without my help.

Earl, one year later, months after their harvest: "Chester. Me and Amalia and Thalia have talked, and I've got to tell you the truth. Amalia and Thalia argue about which variety of garlic is the best, whatever that means. Me? One variety burns my tongue, another variety burns it less. Then, the next day, the one that burned less yesterday burns more today. I just love the taste of any garlic I use no matter the variety."

Chester: "Earl, I can not, will not, pretend to tell you which garlic is better than another. We all have different body chemistries. What's hot for me might be mild for you, what's mild for you might be hot for me. And identify by appearance? All anyone can say with fair certainty is whether

The Tasting (Yuck!)

this or that garlic is a softneck or a hardneck garlic. I defy the most scientific garlic professor to identify by name and/or country of origin one out of five bulbs I show him. Taste is like beauty. It is in the eye of the beholden."

Amalia: "I told Earl that the night he met me."

Earl: "Here. I'm left-handed. I trust these three I've got in my left hand."

Thalia: "Let's plant those three varieties. I'll write down their names and plant the same ones every autumn for the next ninety-seven years."

That was three years ago.

Last week, when Earl called to remind me of the wine-tasting coming up that evening, he said, "Remember, Chester, Fifteen famous people are gonna be here from America and Asia and Europe and the Antarctic. And those reporters from PBS and NPR and CNN. I got your garlic poster framed. It's on the wall of our dining room. In front of the wines we'll be tasting. Every man and woman and goldfish in the room is gonna wanta buy a copy of that poster. PBS and NPR and CNN will be inviting you on their programs. You'll become famous, and you'll become a millionaire. You want to become a millionaire, Chester?"

I said yes in five languages.

The fifteen guests that evening in the small tasting room at the Gladiola Winery: wine-writers from *The New Yorker* and *The New York Times* and Paris and Rome newspapers; owners of famous wineries from Spain and France and Italy; two famous chefs (one from Plate-a-tude, a world-famous Chicago restaurant, the most expensive restaurant in the world, and one from a world-famous Paris restaurant called something like French Bouffant.)

They all arrived at San Francisco Airport at different times but were all picked up by limousines and brought the sixty miles to the Gladiola Winery up north in Sonoma County, ten miles from my home in Occidental. Earl and Amalia and Thalia took turns guiding the famous winos through the fields and in and out of the dining room and into, finally, immediately after a light dinner, Gladiola Winery's Tasting Room. There, on a table covered with a sky-blue silk cloth, stood eight bottles of wine, the bottles corked and labeled not with names but with numbers.

The NPR and PBS and CNN recording equipment, set up, was waiting. Each guest wine expert rolled his/her eyes and licked his/her chops.

Then came the three same words in four different languages: "Let's do it! ... *Facciamolo!* ... *Faisons-la!* ... *Vamos a hacerlo!*

No need to offer turgid details here. You've seen it all if you go to the movies or you have friends or relatives who can afford expensive restaurants or who read the fancy food and wine magazines or who sneer at beer or Pepsi Cola.

The glazing of eyes and the tensing of arm and leg and gut and ass muscles at the mention of the words *crushing* and *pressing* and *fermentation* and *clarification* and *aging* and *bottling*. The sniffing

The Marriage of Mushrooms & Garlic

of glasses containing the fluid; the rolling of fluid in mouths; the gargling of fluid in the throat, at the back and in the front, or rather, in the front and then the back and then in the middle; the sighs, the gasps, the moans, the meditation, the conversation with God, the tears and the moans and the groans, the near-orgasmic panting and submission to the forces of God who is the Master (Mistress?) wine-maker of The Universe.

No need to record (though, thanks to PBS and NPR and CNN it has all, down to the last comma, been recorded:) " … youthful red … acetic … aroma … oh my God … like I mean … *flavor palate* … Barolo Nebbiolo grape with osso bucho … *vous savez, comme je vous dire* … like I mean oh my God the bouquet … corked … Left Bank Bordeaux … *sai come voglio dire, oh mio Dio* … light bodied … gateway to full body … finish … flabby … middle palate … nose … rich … round … oh my God like … short … *sabes como me rifiero* … *oh mi Dios* … microbiological … chemical … mineral … woody … burnt … nutty … fruity … oh my god like I mean like … citrus … berry … floral … oh my God … spicy … *comme je veux* … like I mean … ."

Thirty three minutes of tri-lingual bullshit.

Bottle after bottle.

Glass after glass.

Spit-into-spittoon after spit-into-spittoon by male or female or gender-neutraled.

And then a trumpet call and silence and—after notes carefully composed and more than just carefully tabulated are recorded—another trumpet call, and the long silence is filled suddenly by the tenor-nearly-alto voice of the Chairman of the American Academy of Wines: "The unanimous choice for Best in the House, my Fellow Lovers, is Bottle Number 3! Mr. Gladiola, the winner, please."

Earl, saluting each of the four prostrate bodies on the floor: "Bottle Number 3 is … my God. No, not God. It's … bottle Number 3 is Gladiola Winery's Natalia Ottimo!"

Earl, at seven a.m. the next day, after every guest had departed San Francisco Airport, is on my phone. "Know what, Chester?"

"What, Earl? Oh, congratulations. You are now a very wealthy man and Gladiola Wines will sell for … ."

"Prices of both wines will remain the same, Chester. But you gotta know … ."

Silence.

"Know what, Earl?

"You gotta know what did it, Chester?"

"What did it?"

"Did you taste it in the wine in Bottle three, Chester?"

"Taste what in the wine, Earl?"

"The garlic."

"The garlic? You had garlic in that wine?"

The Tasting (Yuck!)

"Thalia did it. Three cloves of Red Toch. Pressed into the wine when it was bottled sixteen hours and twelve minutes and four seconds before the tasting began."

"Earl, I didn't hear what you just said."

"I didn't say it, Chester. But now everyone's gone, and they can't hear me, and there's no record of it being done, I can tell you."

"Earl, the next time … ."

"The next time is not ever gonna be, Chester. Excuse me. I got a call here on my dumb-ass smart phone from someone at PBS. Talk to you later. But you speak Hebrew, right?"

"Hardly."

"Well, I've been wonderin'. You know how you say *Quelle* Bull Shit! in Hebrew?"

"Let me get back to you on that, Earl. I'll check out Google Translate."

"I'll get Thalia to do that. She's good on a computer."

The Marriage of Mushrooms & Garlic

Brown (and White) Clamshell Mushroom

AKA Beech mushroom, buna shimeji and by its scientific name *Hysozygus mainarius*.

Buna is a Japanese word meaning *beech*. This mushroom is indigenous to Japan and some other northern Asian countries.

This cute little mushroom is also very special to me, especially the alba (white) variety.

More than twenty years ago, while on a trip to Japan, I spotted a new mushroom in the fresh produce section of a supermarket. It was obvious to me that it had been cultivated in what is referred to as the bottle method. The telltale circular marks at the base of the stems were a dead giveaway.

So, with the mindset of "if they can do it, I can do it," I purchased the pack and took them back to Dr. Yoshii's lab.

Equipped with all the right instruments, I soon had several agar test tubes with this mushroom's tissue culture and prepared them for carrying back to California. On arrival, I, as always,

declared it to agricultural inspection. The expression on the new face of a young inspector seemed very suspicious. He called over his supervisor, who, on spotting me, said "Oh, it's the mushroom man. What have you got this time?"

He gave the tubes a quick glance and said, "Thank you for declaring. Please go ahead."

So, my little *Hipsozygus marinarius* had a new home and soon a new name. It was even going to have a kind of sibling.

As there was no available information on how to cultivate this mushroom, I was going to have to develop my own cultivation processes. Having been in this situation before and having succeeded, I was confident I could do this.

Using fresh new tissue cultures from the supermarket specimens, it was only six months before we had a controlled process. A little more perfecting, and this mushroom would go into full production; and that we did. Soon, we were marketing a tasty new mushroom with a new name (thanks to my naming committee). We named it the brown clamshell mushroom—it reminded me of the little brown-mottled clams we used to collect as kids, and it had a hint of shellfish in its flavor.

But that's not the end of this success story. Two or three years into production, while doing my daily inspection of the harvest rooms, I spotted a pure white mushroom growing in the middle of a batch of the regular brown ones. What I had found was a clam-shell mushroom without pigment—in simple terms, an albino.

So, again off to the lab, where it was tissue-cultured and allowed to develop. With my fingers crossed that it would stay true and remain white, I waited.

When the little primordia (baby mushrooms) started growing, they were, indeed, white.

We named it the alba clamshell mushroom, and it was a big success. Some chefs even preferred it over its brown sibling, saying that it tasted even nicer. I would agree, but said, "Yes, but you know that it costs more."

After a year or two of almost total exclusivity, the alba was cultivated by other growers and is now grown on a large scale in Japan, Korea, China, Taiwan, Thailand and, of course, the USA.

The Marriage of Mushrooms & Garlic

Clamshell Mushroom Recipes

PESTO ALFREDO
WITH MUSHROOMS AND GARLIC

8 ounces of dry penne or rigatoni pasta
1 pound of brown clamshell mushrooms
4 tbsps. butter divided
$^3/_4$ C. cream at room temperature
$^1/_3$ C. grated Parmesan or pecorino cheese
4 cloves minced garlic
salt and white pepper to taste

Sauté the mushrooms in 2 tbsp. of the butter on medium heat. When golden and caramelized, sprinkle with some salt, toss and set aside. Cook the pasta until al dente. Drain and return to the pot with the remaining butter and stir until coated with the butter. Add the cream, grated cheese, minced garlic, and mushrooms and toss well to combine. Add salt and pepper to taste. Serve immediately, garnished with a little more of the grated cheese.

CRUSTLESS MUSHROOM AND GARLIC QUICHE

1 pound of brown clamshell mushrooms
2 tbsp. butter
4 eggs
1 1/2 c of half & half
1 c of grated Swiss cheese
1 tsp. salt
1 tsp. nutmeg
3 cloves of garlic slivered lengthwise

Sauté the mushrooms in the butter until golden and caramelized. Set aside. Beat together all of the remaining ingredients except for the garlic to make a "custard." Place the cooked mushrooms in the bottom of a large buttered pie plate and cover with the custard. Bake in a preheated 375° oven for 20 minutes. Remove from the oven and place the garlic slivers evenly over the quiche. Return to oven and bake until golden brown on top and firm when jiggled. Allow to sit at room temperature for 15 minutes before serving.

The Marriage of Mushrooms & Garlic

CREAMED MUSHROOMS ON TOAST POINTS

2 slices of bread
1 pound brown clamshell mushrooms
3 cloves minced garlic
4 tbsp. butter
3 tbsp. flour
1¹/₂ C. half & half
2 tbsp. cream sherry or to taste
Salt and white pepper to taste

Toast and butter the bread and slice each piece into 4 triangles. Place the triangles onto a serving platter with some of the toast points facing out in a "star" pattern and set aside. Melt the butter in a large skillet and sauté the mushrooms until they start to turn golden on the edges. Add the garlic. Add the flour and stir well to combine. Add the half & half and cook on medium heat until bubbling and thickened. Turn heat to low and add the sherry to your taste. Add salt and pepper to taste. Pour the mushroom mixture over the center of the toast points leaving the tips of the toast points showing. Serve immediately.

Clamshell Mushroom Recipes

GROUND PORK SALAD WITH MUSHROOM (MOO NAM-SOD)

The blend of fresh herbs and lime juice makes this salad very refreshing. This recipe is popular with the people in the central region of Thailand. Other meat, such as chicken, can also be used.

3/4 pound ground/minced pork loin
1/2 pound chopped clamshell mushrooms
3 tbsp. fish sauce
2 tbsp. fresh lime juice
2 tbsp. thinly sliced shallot
2 tbsp. chopped fresh ginger
1 tbsp. chopped green onion
1 tbsp. chopped cilantro
1/2 C. toasted peanut
1/2 tsp. dry ground roasted red Thai chili pepper
1/2 tsp. fresh minced garlic
2 tbsp. cooking oil
10 leaves of red lettuce or romaine lettuce

Combine the ground pork with fish sauce and 3 tbsp. of water in the skillet.

Heat the skillet and cook the mixture on medium heat for 5 minutes or until the pork is cooked, stirring to break up the meat. Remove the skillet from the heat and set on the side to cool down.

In a second skillet, cook the garlic in oil on medium heat. Stir in the mushrooms and cook for 5 minutes. Remove the skillet and set aside to cool down.

When both mixtures are cool, combine with lime juice, chili powder and add the chopped green onion, cilantro, toasted peanuts and ginger. Mix thoroughly so that everything is well combined.

Serve with raw vegetables, such as red leaf lettuce or romaine lettuce, by using the leaf as a wrapper for the mixture.

❖ ❖ ❖

The Marriage of Mushrooms & Garlic

HOT AND SOUR SOUP WITH MUSHROOM AND PRAWNS (TOM YUM GOONG)

A subtle blend of spicy hot and sour with citrus overtones, tom yum goong is the most famous of Thai soups. Each region has its own particular variation of the recipe.

8 ounces prawns (or shrimp), shelled and
   deveined, with shells reserved
3 C. water
5 keffir lime leaves
3 thin slices fresh galangal
2 stalks lemongrass, lower $^2/_3$ portion only, cut
   into 1-inch lengths
$^1/_4$ C. fish sauce
1 C. sliced clamshell mushrooms
1 tsp. chopped fresh Thai chili

$^1/_4$ C. fresh lime juice
1 tbsp. chopped cilantro

Take the prawn shells, lime leaves, galangal, fish sauce, lemongrass and place them in a pot with water. Heat to boiling for 5 minutes then strain the broth.

Place the broth in the pot; add mushrooms and boil for 3 minutes.

Add the prawns to the soup, and reheat to a gentle boil. When the prawns are cooked, place the lime juice and chili in a serving bowl, stir, garnish with cilantro, and serve.

Clamshell Mushroom Recipes

MISO SALMON WITH CLAMSHELL MUSHROOM

Hokkaido-style salmon adapted by Pic. This dish contains the authentic flavors of Japan. It is delicious and easy to prepare with a tantalizing presentation.

1 c white miso paste
1 c white sugar
3 tbsp. sake (if not available, substitute white wine, Madeira, or sherry wine)
2-pound fillet of salmon
1 tbsp. chopped fresh garlic
1 pound fresh clamshell mushroom
1/8 tsp. black ground pepper
1 tbsp. of soy sauce
3 tbsp. of cooking oil

Mix miso paste, sugar and sake, set aside.

Pat dry and place salmon on baking pan. Spread a thin layer (about 1/8 inch) of the miso paste mix to cover the salmon.

Bake the salmon at 450° F for 10 minutes. Switch to broil for 5 minutes to brown it.

Heat the skillet and cook the garlic in oil on medium heat. Stir in the mushrooms, cook for 5 minutes. Add soy sauce and black pepper.

Serve the salmon and garnish with mushrooms on the side.

The Marriage of Mushrooms & Garlic

CREAMED MUSHROOMS AND PEAS IN PUFF PASTRY SHELLS

1 package of frozen puff pastry shells
1 pound of alba clamshell mushrooms
2 cloves of garlic
3 tbsp. butter
1 package of frozen peas
$^1/_4$ C. of flour
$1^1/_2$ C. of milk
2 tbsp. cream sherry
salt and white pepper to taste

Prepare the puff pastry shells according to the package directions and set aside. Sauté the mushrooms and garlic in the butter until cooked through but not browned. Sprinkle with the flour and stir to combine. Add the milk and simmer on low until thickened. Add the peas and cook until the peas are heated through. Add the salt and pepper to taste. Add the sherry and sample to adjust seasoning and sherry to your liking. Spoon into the puff pastry shells and serve immediately.

37

Clamshell Mushroom Recipes

CREAMY POLENTA
WITH MUSHROOMS AND GARLIC

4 tbsp. butter
1 pound of alba mushrooms
3 cloves minced garlic
1 medium yellow onion
1 tbsp. dried oregano or herbs d Provence
$^1/_2$ c vermouth
1 c of coarse grain polenta
4 tbsp. butter
$^1/_2$ c grated Parmesan cheese
$^1/_4$ c mascarpone cheese
salt to taste
2 tbsp. chopped parsley

Melt the butter in a large heavy-bottomed skillet. Sauté the mushrooms until golden and caramelized. Add the garlic, onion and herbs and cook on low until onion and garlic are done. Add vermouth and stir well to combine. Cover and keep warm in a low oven. Melt the additional 4 tbsp. of butter in a large saucepan. Add the dry polenta and stir well to coat all of the grains with butter. Add 6 cups of boiling water and cook on low until polenta is soft and creamy. Add salt to taste. Stir in Parmesan and mascarpone cheeses. Spoon polenta onto a large platter. Remove mushrooms from oven and spoon on top of polenta. Sprinkle with chopped parsley.

❖ ❖ ❖

The Marriage of Mushrooms & Garlic

WILD RICE WITH MUSHROOMS AND GARLIC

1 C. of wild rice
1 onion, chopped
2 C. of chicken or vegetable broth
1 tsp. salt
1 pound of alba clamshell mushrooms
2 tbsp. butter
4 cloves garlic

Soak the wild rice in the broth for 2 hours or more. While rice is soaking, sauté the mushrooms in the butter until golden and caramelized. Set aside. Add the remaining cup of broth to the rice and add the chopped onion. Bring to a boil on medium heat and simmer on low until the level of the broth is even with the top of the rice and small "volcanoes" have formed. Add the mushrooms, garlic and salt and stir to combine. Cover with a lid and allow to simmer on low until water is completely evaporated. Turn off heat and allow to sit with lid on about 10 minutes more. Serve immediately.

Clamshell Mushroom Recipes

The Garlic-Is-Life Festival

Darrell Merrell of Tulsa, Oklahoma guided me (I was then in my mid-seventies) into my role of international garlic guru. As a result, Darrell became not just a dear friend but a confidante and soul-mate. We called each other on the phone and e-mailed each other and visited each other for almost ten years, until I found traveling even as far as my bathroom too demanding a task.

Darrell, a sixty-eight year-old youth, died in Tulsa in May 2008. He had been a garlic lover for less than ten years. An intense garlic lover. By accident.

It came about in the late 1990s.

He had been caring for his sister and his mother, and both sister and mother died. Darrell, needing income, did not want to return to his earlier life as a stockbroker and businessman. As he said to me once when he traveled to California to visit me, "I needed ties not to heaven but to earth, so I started growing tomatoes. And selling them."

Darrell, then peddling books every Saturday at the Tulsa Flea Market, started selling the type of tomato he was then growing in his backyard garden for himself and his daughter Lisa.

"It dawned on me that if gardeners could get the type of tomatoes I was growing and eating, they would love them just like Lisa and me loved them. The nurseries were selling hybrids, and hybrids don't have the flavor of the old-time, open-pollinated heirloom varieties I was growing."

Very soon, he was selling far more tomatoes than books. The more tomatoes he sold, the more tomatoes he grew.

One Saturday, on the "front porch" of the Tulsa Flea Market, held at the fairgrounds, Darrell was discovered and praised by Tulsa resident and media star Karen Keith. Karen, for years, had been offering live broadcasts on the *Tulsa Home and Garden Show* and the KJRH-2 *Early Morning Show.*

With Karen Keith as midwife, Darrell Merrell the Tomato Man was born.

In 1995, as a favor to his friend Charles Shaver, Darrell purchased five heirloom varieties of so-called gourmet garlic from that friend. In the single month after my first harvest of those

gourmet garlics, I ate more garlic than I'd eaten in the two hundred years I'd lived before nine-teen-ninety-five," Darrell told me when he called me in California on September 9, 1998. "I was hooked. Then I met you and knew five minutes after we started talking on the telephone that day you were gonna be my daddy and mommy and brother and sister and friend all combined. You are family, Chester."

"How'd you happen to get my name, Darrell?"

"I didn't get you, you got me, Chester. I had a tattered copy of your book called Garlic is Life for sale, and I started reading it one day and sat there and read it beginning to end. My daughter Lisa dealt with the customers. I just read it first page to last page."

"That book Garlic is Life changed my life, Chester."

That first phone call lasted for about an hour. Darrell then bought a copy of my beautiful garlic poster.

The Marriage of Mushrooms & Garlic

Home was a farmhouse filled wall-to-wall and ceiling-to-floor with boxes of books and magazines and plants and straw hats and shoes and kitty cats. I couldn't get near the poster to autograph it when I eventually was able to visit, so Darrell carried it outside onto the porch one day, and I autographed it, and he rolled it up and kissed it and took it inside and leaned it, rolled up, against the wall.

When I told Darrell I had been in Tulsa during the war but had not had reason to ever return again, he said, "Chester, you're gonna have a reason now. I'm gonna set up a garlic festival here in Tulsa, and you're gonna be the guest of honor. Our festival will make every other garlic festival in the country look like a comic book. How about it?"

Being sure it would never happen and I would never have to get on the plane, I accepted the invitation.

The first Garlic Is Life Festival and Symposium was held in Tulsa October 14–16, 1999. The Second Annual Garlic Is Life Festival and Symposium was held October 10–14, 2000, and the third and last Annual Garlic Is Life Festival and Symposium was held October 30–November 3, 2001. Thanks again to Karen Keith and to the *Tulsa World* newspaper and to the University of Oklahoma, over those three years I met farmers and writers and professors and chefs and artists from all over the world.

Now, these days, when I think of family, I see and hear the faces and voices of Darrell Merrell and Lisa Merrell and Bob Anderson and Linda and Doug Urig and … and … and … and …

Darrell's prediction came true.

Those three Garlic Is Life Symposiums and Festivals changed the nation's and the world's attitudes toward that magnificent herb to which I had been introduced my father.

People from all over the nation and then the world began calling me, writing me, e-mailing. Virtually every contact began with the same words: "Hello, are you the Garlic Guy?"

Enough of me about me.

It is time now for Bob Anderson of Bangs, Texas, to take over. On my request, Bob submitted the following information.

My name is Bob Anderson, and I run one of the most popular garlic websites on the Internet.

Darrell Merrell was one of the most important people in determining how the last part of my life is turning out, due directly to things I learned and people I met year after year at the Garlic is Life Symposium and Festival.

At first, in 1997, Darrell did not get involved with computers or the Internet, but a friend of his saw my website and said, "Wow! I never knew there were so many different kinds of garlic, and all different." He printed out my website, which

The Garlic-Is-Life Festival

was a lot smaller back then, and gave it to Darrell, who read it and said "Wow! I never knew there were so many kinds of garlic, and all different."

He immediately ordered 26 cultivars from me.

When Darrell finally read my website, he liked not only the plethora of garlic information about every aspect of garlic but he also liked my folksy, friendly presentation. Occasionally, in our phone conversations and e-mails, he tended to get a little poetic about the spiritual aspect of spending most of your time outside in the presence of God, however one perceives God to be.

Darrell was a big, tall, friendly fat man with a big, quick grin who didn't have a shy corpuscle in his body. We talked about garlic and life in general.

One day in late 1998 or early 1999, he called and told me he had decided to host a three-day combination scientific symposium and garlic festival there in Tulsa and invited me to attend as a vendor. I had doubts about whether Tulsa had the demographic to support all that, but I jumped at it anyway and committed fully to it because it had not been done before and because I wanted to learn all I could from knowledgeable people.

The Garlic is Life Symposium and Festival was unlike any other garlic festival I had ever attended anywhere in the United States. It was the two days of lectures from invited experts that set it apart.

From the beginning, it was intended to be more of an information exchange than a merry-making festival, but the intent was to sell enough garlic to finance the whole affair.

Alas, it fell short in that category, as sales were simply never enough; and it went into the red, and Darrell wound up paying for it out of his own pocket.

Over the next three years, there were three symposia and festivals with seminars; and Darrell named them the Garlic is Life Symposium and Festival after Chester Aaron's book of that name: *Garlic is Life*.

Chester was always the guest of honor at all of the events.

The lectures were presented on Thursday and Friday and the festival on Saturday. Speakers would arrive on Wednesday and spend the day meeting one another and touring some local features and having dinner together with the idea of getting to know each other. The group chose to take all meals together so they would have more time to talk and compare notes.

These were widely separated people who rarely, if ever, are able to talk with anyone on their level; and when brought together, they suddenly found lots of people they could talk shop with. For me and many many others, it was a dream come true.

The Marriage of Mushrooms & Garlic

The garlic conversations among experts took place at every spare moment they had. Never before or since have such conversations about farming in general and garlic in particular taken place.

As informative as the lectures were, it was the question-and-answer sessions at the end of the lectures where the most pertinent questions were asked and answered. I learned more in the conversations during coffee breaks and lunches by keeping quiet and listening and making some tablet notes and a lot of mental notes.

For me, the dinners every evening were the best. Based on the random seating, you never knew who your conversation partners were going to be, but you always knew what the conversation was going to be about.

One evening we had reservations for about 35 people at this really upscale Tulsa restaurant with plush carpeting, subdued lighting and candles, starched linen tablecloths and napkins, real silverware and all the accoutrements of fine dining in a sophisticated setting. You can bet hamburger wasn't on the menu.

As soon as we were seated, they served us hard rolls and butter; and on each table there were large bulbs of red toch, a rich, musky, earthy garlic with only a mild bite.

We all ate raw garlic and hard rolls while we waited for our food. A special garlic wine was served with the meal. The floor and tables in our whole area were covered in garlic skins, and the conversation soared.

The Garlic-Is-Life Festival

At first, people didn't know how to take this, until they realized how much fun we were having; and the waiters and other patrons all laughed with us, and we even shared the garlic with a few other diners.

An important thing to understand is that when people eat garlic, especially raw, it has physical effects. It makes people feel good and gives them energy because it contains significant amounts of adenosine triphosphatease (ATP), which the body uses to release energy and make one feel good. This is what is referred to as a garlic high.

When you get people on a garlic high together, they instantly like each other. Conversations last for days, lifetime friendships are formed.

Maybe we ought to feed the diplomatic bigwigs garlic before big summit meetings.

At dinner one evening, my dinner partner was David Mirelman, PhD, Chemistry Chair at Weitzman Institute in Rehovot, Israel. I learned a great secret that changed my life that night.

David explained to me how the allicin in crushed raw non-irradiated garlic killed all bacterial cells and why bacteria, even the most resistant strains like MRSA and MDRTB could not become resistant to garlic. David's explanations, and the discussions I have had with Larry Lawson, PhD, have opened my eyes to how garlic works in the human body.

Without the symposium, I could never have learned these things, which have not been widely published. Much of this information has been incorporated into the Health Benefits of Garlic and the Garlic Pills and Oils pages of my website. Anyone who visits my site can be informed.

Each symposium was bigger and better than the previous, with the 2001 being the best. What is hard to put into words is the atmosphere that permeated each symposium. There was an aura of warmth, friendship and camaraderie, great expectations and a happy glow from the copious amounts of red toch consumed. Chester Aaron once said that red toch was his favorite garlic. It was a sentimental favorite because it came from the village in Georgia where his father was born.

There was no symposium in 2002, but there was a finale in 2003 that was really special. Two distinguished scientists announced a DNA botanical classification of garlic. Those two scientists—Gayle Volk, PhD, of the USDA in Colorado, and Joachim Keller, PhD, of the Plant Institute of Gaterslaben, Germany—had conducted the same type of research and had come to the same conclusions about the classification of garlic and our modern understanding of the classifications.

The Marriage of Mushrooms & Garlic

Over the three years and three symposia I attended dozens of well-structured, well-presented lectures on many topics, of interest only to garlic lovers who wanted to know all the details. I listened to famous cookbook authors such as Fred and Linda Griffith, who wrote *Garlic, Garlic, Garlic*, and Louis and Marie Van Deven, who wrote *Onions and Garlic Forever*. I sampled garlic preparations by many expert chefs like William Woys Weaver, well-known author and food authority, and Tony Lia, former chef at the Stinking Rose restaurant (I incorporated some of these things into the Cooking Tips page on my website.)

At every symposium, Friday night was Garlic Feast Night, as Darrell had arranged for a huge feast with up to 16 chefs. They each prepared their own garlicky specialties at cooking stations set up all around a huge meeting room, and diners could go from station to station and have their dishes prepared for them right on the spot while they watched and chatted with the chefs. The heady aromas of so much garlic being cooked all around the room gave the feast an almost palpable air, and belly dancers performed after dinner to lend a Mediterranean atmosphere.

I learned more about the chemistry of garlic at those three symposia than I could possibly have learned anywhere else. I learned, for example, what makes some garlics taste oniony and others like mustard or horseradish, thanks to Dr. Bill Randall of the University of Georgia.

At one of the festivals, I bought Larry Lawson's book *Garlic, The Science and Therapeutic Application of Allium Sativum L. and Related Species* and got him to autograph it for me. It is the most comprehensive book ever written about the chemistry of garlic, and much of the information on my website about the chemistry of garlic and garlic pills and oils came from applying the information in this book to real life and learning to use it in different ways to get better results.

But there is a lot more to garlic than just eating it.

One theme that ran consistently throughout all of the symposia and among all the attendees was a profound love and respect for both Chester Aaron and Darrell Merrell, who were thoroughly admired by all.

The symposia were the greatest gatherings of garlic intelligentsia ever. Meaningful information passed along continuously wherever any two people would meet. We all became instant old friends.

I am no longer a commercial garlic grower, although I still grow a small quantity for family use and to preserve a few rare cultivars. However, I have opened up an online farmers market on my website to allow small sustainable growers from all over the country to take advantage of my site's high position in the search engine rankings to sell their garlic to a national audience. I'm enabling people to use the Internet to make money from home, anywhere from a few thousand dollars to a lot of thousands, depending on what one has to offer. Right now, I have 15 or 20 different growers from all across the country with garlics people can buy direct, and several more are ready to be added.

The Garlic is Life Symposia and Festivals are but fond memories that are slipping away with the sands of time; but for a while there, the things that were said and done in Tulsa were like a stone thrown into a calm pond, a stone that produced ripples all out of proportion to its size.

Unfortunately, Darrell Merrell has passed away, and no one has arisen to take his place. He was personally responsible for the creation and life of this unique gathering, and he will reside forever in my personal hall of fame not only for the things I learned and the people I met there but also for the love and acceptance I felt there. Some parts of the emotional high lasted for a few days and others for a few weeks, gradually giving way to the hubbub of the busy late-summer to mid-fall garlic season.

Could it happen again? I would love to see it happen again, but I'm not sure it could. While the material is fascinating to the few of us who love garlic, the average person would feel slightly interested but probably not enough to travel to attend and incur the expense of a hotel and eating out and also paying an admission fee. Holding it in a different city each year in conjunction with a local garlic festival might be an option.

Even if the symposium could rise from its own ashes like the phoenix, it would never be the same as the Garlic is Life Symposium. That was Camelot. The way it was can only be revisited at my website, since that seems to be the only place that remembers these historic gatherings. I will preserve their memory as long as I can, for the great friendships, all of the great information exchanges, garlicky atmosphere, great meals proved to be worth remembering and preserving.

Please go to www.gourmetgarlicgardens.com/garlicislife.htm/ to read the details of each conference and see the pictures of the people involved.

The Marriage of Mushrooms & Garlic

Hen of the Woods (Maitake) Mushroom

Although its scientific name is *Grifola fondosa*, the name *maitake* is becoming more and more popular as this mushroom's availability increases. In fact, more people know it *only* as maitake because of some very visible health food/functional food product articles and marketing.

The word *maitake* basically means "dancing mushroom," as the Japanese who found this rare and tasty mushroom would dance with joy. I've often visualized a group of middle-aged Japanese women in their casual working kimonos dancing in a circle around a poor little maitake that soon will be in the pot.

Most mushroom books will have it listed under hen of the woods or *Grifola frondosa*.

It is a strange-looking mushroom and is probably so named because it appears as though it has the overlapping feathers of a bird. It's found in northern Asia, Europe and North America. I have found it growing as far north as the Maskoka Lake district of Ontario, Canada.

I have successfully cultivated it after taking culture from several different variants, my favorite being one that grows east of the Rocky Mountains. It is a far more robust variety and, in my opinion, offers a nicer flavor. I never achieved the comfort level of substantial cultivation.

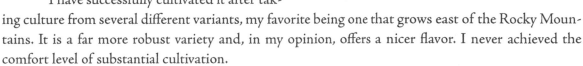

By far the most successful cultivation was achieved by the Japanese, and they currently produce it on a massive scale. They export to North America and Europe and have even set up a production facility in the US Korea and China are not far behind, and there are several small growers in the US, including Gourmet Mushrooms Inc., that grow them under the more desirable organic standards.

It can now be enjoyed in many fine restaurants in very creative dishes. My favorite is a simple Japanese dish callled maitake gohan.

MEDICINAL VALUES

There is a lot of research going on with maitake, and there are several nutriceutical products on the market that are being successfully marketed. Reputed to have unique anti-viral polysaccharides, it is available online and in health food stores in tablet and capsule form.

Hen of the Woods (Maitake) Mushroom Recipes

BRUSCHETTA WITH MAITAKE MUSHROOMS AND GARLIC

1 loaf of rustic French bread
3 tbsp. butter
1 pound of maitake mushrooms
3 cloves minced garlic
salt to taste
1 large clove of whole garlic
olive oil for drizzling
shaved Parmesan cheese

Separate the maitake mushrooms into "sprigs" and saute in the butter until golden and caramelized. Add the garlic and salt to taste and stir to blend. Slice the bread and toast or grill the slices. Slice the whole garlic in half and rub the cut side on the top of each piece of toast. Mound some of the mushrooms on top of each slice of bread and drizzle with olive oil. Scatter with shaved Parmesan.

MAITAKE MUSHROOM GOHAN (RICE)

The blend of maitake mushroom and steamed rice makes this a simple and tasty dish to make.

1 pound maitake mushrooms
3 tbsp. vegetable oil
3 tbsp. soy sauce
2 tbsp. sugar
3 C. short grain rice

Cook the rice and set aside.

Prepare the maitake mushroom in the food processor or cut into very small pieces.

Heat the oil in the pan. Stir-fry the mushrooms over high heat for 5 minutes, stirring continuously.

Add soy sauce and sugar. Stir well to combine all ingredients. Remove from the heat.

Combine the cooked rice and the mushrooms into a mixing bowl, mix well and serve.

The Marriage of Mushrooms & Garlic

Trumpet Royale Mushroom

AKA king oyster, eringii mushroom and by its scientific name *Plurotus eryngii*.

This very popular mushroom is now cultivated in most parts of the world, and that popularity has really only happened in about the last fifteen years or so. Its original home is in the Middle East, but talented researchers in Japan brought this versatile mushroom into the culinary limelight.

As in the previous cases, I spotted this mushroom in a supermarket in Japan. I purchased a small packet of the freshest ones I could see, and they returned with me to California a few days later. I was able to tissue-culture it so that I now had the means to replicate it as many times as was necessary until I was able to produce some interesting fruit bodies.

This is a fascinating mushroom and very handsome as well. It proved to be quite challenging to get it to do what we wanted in the way of shape and economical yield (volume of harvest). However, we were spurred on by the fact that this mushroom had all the necessary credentials to make it on the gourmet list—taste, shelf life, handsome appearance—and not least because no one else was growing it in North America, perhaps even in the Western Hemisphere.

I needed to give it a name that would be easy on the tongue and look good on a menu and the label on a packet. So, as in the past, the mushroom was prepared in several dishes, and with my trusty naming committee friends Dee, Dennis, Richard, Michael, and Pic, I sat down and examined, tasted and debated. After a long evening, we all finally decided in favor of the rather regal-sounding name the "trumpet royal."

Several months later, I had a viable cultivation method; and we plugged it in to grow it on a larger scale. The gourmet market welcomed it and demand took off. Today, it is cultivated in many countries, used in restaurants, and found in supermarkets around the world.

The Marriage of Mushrooms & Garlic

Trumpet Royale Mushroom Recipes

RATATOUILLE

1 large zucchini
1 large onion
1 pound trumpet mushrooms
1 large eggplant
1 green pepper
1 large vine ripened tomato
6 minced garlic cloves
$^1/_4$ C. of olive oil
2 tsp. oregano
salt and pepper to taste
Grated parmesan cheese

Cube all of the vegetables into approximately $^1/_2$- to $^3/_4$-inch chunks. Pour the olive oil into a large heavy skillet and heat until almost hot. Add all of the vegetables except the tomatoes and sauté on medium heat until done. Add the minced garlic, oregano and tomatoes. Turn heat to low and simmer for another 10 minutes or so and add salt and pepper to taste. Serve immediately with a generous dusting of the Parmesan cheese.

CREAMED LEEKS
WITH MUSHROOMS AND GARLIC

4 tbsp. butter
Cooking oil
3 large leeks
1 pound of trumpet mushrooms
2 cloves minced garlic
1/4 C. flour
2 C. half & half
1 tsp. nutmeg
salt and white pepper to taste

Slice a 2-inch piece off one of the leeks. Cut this piece lengthwise into matchstick-sized slivers. Heat a small cast iron skillet and add the cooking oil to a depth of about 1/4 inch.

When the oil is hot, scatter the slivered leeks into it and cook, stirring, until golden brown. Drain on paper towels and set aside.

Slice the remainder of the leeks and the trumpet mushrooms into 1/4-inch slices. Sauté them in the butter until soft and translucent. Add the minced garlic and sprinkle with the flour. Stir to combine well and add the half & half. Cook on medium heat until bubbling and thickened. Adjust heat to low and add the nutmeg and salt and pepper to taste.

Pour onto a serving platter and garnish with the fried leek slivers. Serve immediately.

❖ ❖ ❖

The Marriage of Mushrooms & Garlic

TRUMPET ROYALE MUSHROOMS WITH SWEET THAI CHILE PASTE

The combination of trumpet mushrooms and sweet chile paste makes this a simple and tasty dish to make.

2 pound trumpet mushrooms sliced to $^1/_4$ inch thick
3 tbsp. vegetable oil
2 tbsp. chopped fresh basil
2 tbsp. sweet Thai chile paste (Pantainorasingn brand)
pinch of salt and black pepper

Heat the oil in the pan. Stir-fry the mushrooms over high heat for 5 minutes, stirring continuously. Add sweet Thai chile paste, salt and black pepper. Stir well to combine all ingredients, cook about 3 minutes, stir in fresh basil, remove from heat and serve.

Teeny Biaggio

*G*arlic Kisses is a collection of stories about the people I met during the thirty years I was a garlic farmer. The book was originally published in 1931 by Doug Urig (Mostly Garlic Ltd.) and then republished in 2004 by Elizabeth Burton (Zumaya Publications LLC).

The third story in *Garlic Kisses* is about Crystal Biaggio. Time of the occurrence of the events in that story: 1997.

Fifteen years ago.

I was seventy-four years young. Crystal was eleven years old.

The fifth-grade teacher at Deep Creek Middle School, Mrs. Apperson, had called me one morning in September two weeks after classes started to request my consent to an interview by a student named Crystal Biaggio.

"The assignment for each of the fifteen students in this class," the teacher said, "is to interview someone local who is famous. Crystal informed me that Chester Aaron is local and he is a famous garlic guy and he is her friend. I am familiar with your name, Mr. Aaron. Several years ago, I was a teacher at Murray Middle School in San Francisco. Your young-adult novels in our library were much admired by teachers and students. I must confess I have not read your garlic books. I am allergic to garlic."

I had no reason to inform Mrs. Apperson that, although I had known the Biaggios (mother, father, daughter) for years, I thought of them as friends but not close friends. We shared neighbors with whom we, the Biaggios and I, had dined two times at the Union Hotel in Occidental. Crystal had accompanied her parents at those two meals, and at each meal, I was more than just charmed by the tough but gleeful cherub's intelligence and her curiosity about my having published short stories and novels. One question I still remember: "Chester, is a novel a book or is a book a novel or is a novel just a long, long short story?"

Having retired from Saint Catherine's College three years before Crystal had been born, I had no difficulty resisting the impulse to pontificate in my response. Crystal's father Tony, a plumber, and her mother Bianca, a legal secretary, and our neighbors (occupations and interests varied then and now), pretended not to be bored.

The day and hour for my interview by Crystal was set for the Friday following Mrs. Apperson's call. Crystal's mother brought her to my farm at exactly four o'clock. The late-afternoon breeze was so warm the three of us sat outside on the deck, on redwood chairs surrounding a long redwood table. From there we could view the western field and the sixty boxes in which, for the past month, I had been planting that year's crop.

Each of fifty-nine of the sixty boxes was packed with 150 to 200 cloves—eighty different varieties of garlic from more than twenty different countries—and striped with drip-lines that were in turn covered with a blanket of rice straw.

After setting glasses and a pitcher of iced tea and a tray of chocolate chip cookies on the table, I sat back in my chair to let Crystal decide the procedure for the interview.

Crystal laid out on the table the two pages of pertinent questions given her by her teacher, and while sipping iced tea and nibbling cookies, she considered the details on the pages.

"You are a famous writer," she said, setting the pages aside. "Mrs. Apperson said you and your books were written up in the *New York Times* and the *San Francisco Chronicle* and fancy big papers all over the country. Tell me, Chester, what's the word *plot* mean?"

I answered as best I could, and then, for the next half-hour, I responded to one question after another, questions never even asked, years ago, by my Upper Division English majors at Saint Catherine's College.

"What's the difference between a simile and a metaphor, Chester? … When is it better to use a simile than a metaphor, Chester? … Why do most writers make up stories about lives they've never lived, Chester? … Why is every story told by an I-did-this or a he-or-she-did-this or a they-did-this but never a you-did-this?"

It was about five o'clock when Crystal folded her two pages and shoved them down into the back pocket of her patched and faded jeans.

"Okay," she said. "Last question, Chester."

And *bang!*

As if the sound of the name *Chester* had been a signal, two bats leaped out from beneath the eaves and roared past Bianca and me. They skimmed Crystal's face so closely they clipped her eyelashes. Then they zoomed up into the thick green summer-growth of the three-hundred-year-old redwood tree at the side of the deck.

Crystal, screaming, leaped out of her chair and ran. She fell twice, still screaming, before she reached the front door. Once inside the house, she slammed the door and locked it.

I led Bianca around the deck, and we entered the kitchen through the back door. We took turns comforting and reassuring the terrified Crystal until she agreed, finally, to accompany the two

The Marriage of Mushrooms & Garlic

of us out of the house and along the path to their Subaru, parked inside the redwood grove. Her mother walked at Crystal's left side, holding her hand. I walked at her right side, my arm around her shivering shoulders.

"Sorry, Chester," Crystal whispered. "Bats give me itchies in my guts."

After Bianca reminded Crystal to lock her seatbelt, she started the engine.

"Wait," I said, giving Crystal the signal to open her window. "I have an idea, Crystal. How about helping me plant the last of my garlic next week? I have one more box to load. We'll plant about three hundred cloves of a very special garlic."

Crystal looked at her mom, and her mom nodded.

61

"Okay," Crystal said. "But only if you call me Teeny. You calling me Crystal sounds like I'm a character in one of your stories."

"I need your muscle, Teeny. We'll plant the last box with garlic from Transylvania."

"Wow," she whispered. "Transylvania. Garlic from Transylvania. Maybe if I eat garlic from Transylvania, I'll never be attacked by witches or werewolves or maybe even bats."

"I promise you," I said. "Witches and werewolves and bats hate Transylvanian garlic. If you eat Transylvanian garlic, bats and witches and werewolves will never come near you."

Teeny laughed and lifted both arms to display her tiny-bubble biceps.

The following Saturday afternoon, when Bianca Biaggio brought Teeny to my farm, she made one request.

"I'm leaving Crystal with you, Chester. Please bring her home around five o'clock. There's an event at Saint Anne's Church this evening, and we're all three going to it."

"No problema, Bianca."

Teeny: "I didn't know you spoke Transylvanian, Chester."

Of course we all laughed.

For maybe two hours, Teeny—oh, yes, I remembered to use only the name Teeny—worked with shovel and spade and wheelbarrow. She hauled bags of soil supplement from the barn, and we took turns with shovel, rake and spade to mix it into the soil before planting the cloves. I demonstrated in various ways how the cloves had to be planted.

Teeny Biaggio

"Tip up, base down, five to six inches from every other clove, tip about an inch under the topsoil, a teaspoon of this stuff in the hole before the clove goes in ..."

"What's that stuff, Chester?"

"It's a root-feeder. It helps the roots grow and—"

"Would it help me grow if I ate some?"

"Don't think you'd like the smell or the taste, Teeny."

Teeny required one single recital of the clove-planting procedure. As a beginner, she was faster and more efficient than I was. But she was eleven years old.

The Marriage of Mushrooms & Garlic

After the last clove was in the soil and we had arranged the drip-lines, I held up my hand. Teeny slapped her hand into mine.

"*Finito*," she sang.

"*Finito*, indeed, Teeny. Just in time to take you home. But I have a question for you. Do you have any idea what you're been shoveling and hauling in that wheelbarrow?"

"It says soil supplement on the bag," she said.

"It's bat guano."

"Bat gawno?"

"Gwa-no. Bat gwa-no."

"What's bat gwa-no?"

"Bat poop. A very special additive to the soil to help the cloves grow into big solid bulbs."

"You mean bat shit?"

"I mean bat shit."

Teeny, laughing loud and hard, dug her hands down into the crumbs of bat guano remaining in the wheelbarrow, and singing, "Bat shit bat shit bat shit," she threw the crumbs into the air.

"Chester, before you drive me home, can I eat some Transylvanian garlic?"

"You really want to?"

"Yeah. There are mosquitoes at Saint Anne's in the evenings. Mosquitoes eat me like I'm ice cream, and I get puss-bumps all over me. I bet mosquitoes hate Transylvanian garlic."

"Teeny, wait here."

I went into the house, freed two cloves from one of the remaining Transylvanian bulbs and peeled the skin from each clove. Carrying a fresh Gravenstein apple, I returned to the deck, where Teeny, fresh out of the upstairs bathroom, was waiting.

"Transylvanian garlic burns my tongue," I said. "So I eat something sweet with it when I eat it raw. Sweet fruit, for me, cuts the burn to zero. Sometimes I use honey."

Teeny popped the entire raw clove into her mouth and chomped, and her eyes filled with tears. She tried to talk but could only cough and gag. I forced the apple inside her lips and in between her teeth and chomped my own teeth to show her what to do. She took two bites and chewed.

"Wow," she said, shaking the tears from her eyes. "I bet I can kick the ass of the biggest witch ever lived. Come on, you bat shitters!"

"Home you go, Teeny Biaggio."

"That's poetry, Chester. You a poet, too?"

Weeks later, around midsummer, I happened onto Teeny's mother at the Occidental Post Office. She told me Teeny—she said "Crystal," of course—at summer camp, was having fun but enduring her usual summer enemy, the mosquitoes. I asked Bianca for Teeny's address, and the next day I sent her a lotion I have given to several friends who have had severe reactions to

Teeny Biaggio

mosquito bites. A lotion I prepare by crushing a few cloves of one of my spiciest garlics (spiciest for me) into olive oil. This time, for Teeny, the garlic was Transylvanian. I identified the garlic in my cover letter.

Five days later, I received a letter (written in longhand) from Teeny.

"First day all summer I've not been bitten even once. Thanks, Chester. When do you harvest the Transylvania garlic? I helped plant it, so I gotta help harvest it. But can I please maybe buy a few bulbs of Transylvanian garlic and plant it in our garden? Pretty please with garlic on it, Chester?"

That summer, when I harvested my sixty boxes of garlic, Teeny helped me five times.

In September, under my guidance, she and her parents planted thirty cloves of Transylvanian garlic (along with fifteen cloves of each of five other varieties, including three from Italy) in the acreage behind their home in the hills above Occidental.

When I went to my car after the Biaggios fed me the best bruschetta I had ever eaten (even in Italy), Teeny informed me that the garlic on the bruschetta had been the Neapolitan red I had given her. She whispered, so her parents wouldn't hear, that when we'd planted the cloves, it was only the Transylvanian cloves that, before being pushed into the soil precisely as I had taught her—tip up, flat base down—had received a kiss.

"Now," she said, "we won't ever have to buy garlic again. My mom and dad spend about four million dollars a year on garlic, Chester. So we owe you. Goodnight, Chester. You've spun my life in a new direction."

The Biaggios had two acres of level field surrounding their home, and as Teeny entered and progressed through high school, she received possession of those two acres to do with as she pleased. That pleasure: a variety of fruit trees but mainly garlic. Different varieties of garlic.

Using my boxes (each box 5 feet × 10 feet and 24 inches high) as a model, she and her father built two boxes in full sun that first year and then, a year later, two more boxes. Finally, they built the fifth and sixth. Following my advice, Tony Biaggio, to defy the gazillion gophers, lined the floor of each box with wire mesh.

"Gophers must be Italian," Teeny informed me. "They love garlic. You know what Dad calls them? *Terra ratti*. Ground rats."

After graduation from high school, Teeny shrugged off her parents' suggestion that she go to college. She had to give every hour of every day to field work. Bianca informed me that Crystal spent more time in the field than she did in front of the television set or her computer.

"Well, maybe not her computer. She's sitting there every night before she goes to bed. Papers for school, I hope."

Off and on, through the last year in high school, Teeny drove (yes, she now had her license) to my farm without ever preparing me or even requesting permission. There she was suddenly, without a single word of request or assertion, taking the tools and the wheelbarrow from the barn

and digging, weeding, planting, harvesting. If she could find nothing to do in the field involving garlic she would prune my fruit trees or play around with grafting.

"I feel like God when I graft a stock of Indian blood plum to a yellow gem, or a Gravenstein stock to the branch of a Macintosh. Maybe some day I'll graft a gopher to a Border collie and gophers will love garlic and chase sheep."

"You having troubles with gophers this year?"

"Worst ever. But I'm gonna fix it."

"Fix what? What's *it*, Teeny?"

"*It* means the gophers. The *terra ratti*."

And she did fix it.

Teeny succeeded in doing what I and hundreds and thousands of other so-called farmers could never do. She reduced the gopher population to near-zero without the use of traps or guns or poison.

The year after Teeny graduated from high school, she finished (in October) planting a total of 600 garlic cloves in her three boxes. Twelve varieties from eight countries. I had to supply her Transylvanian because almost all of her previous planting had been consumed by gophers before the stalks had reached five inches above the rice straw mulch.

Teeny suggested in late summer that she was going to start planting the first week in September, and she would welcome my help.

"Not because I need any pointers," she said. "I think I know all about garlic—thank you, Chester Aaron. But I want you to see what I'm doing in my war against the *terra ratti*. If it works,

Teeny Biaggio

I'm gonna make a million dollars and take a trip to Italy and Transylvania. Two months in each country. I'll take you with me, Chester."

"What are your weapons in your war against the *terra ratti*, Teeny? You don't have a gun in your house, and you hate to kill even a mosquito, so are you going to pee on the gophers?"

"Come see. No pee-pee."

I went up Coleman Valley Road to Teeny's farm (even her parents now referred to their living on Teeny's farm) and went out into the field with her. She pointed to the five boxes she and her father and I had constructed.

Only now there were seven boxes. All of them packed with garlic cloves, all of them covered with rice-straw mulch (as her master had demanded.) Drip-lines under the straw reached out from the end of one box to the next.

Nothing new, I thought, but then I noticed something new, indeed.

In the four corners of each and every box, and midway down both sides of every box: an empty bottle, pouring end up, each bottle sunk halfway down into the soil under the straw. Bottles of different sizes, different shapes, different origins, but all upright, all uncapped, all empty. Or so I thought.

"What are those?"

"They're bottles."

"Yes, I can see they're bottles, but what are you doing growing bottles?"

"Thanks to those bottles, Chester, I am going to have the best crop ever. I bet I lose maybe ten plants to the *terra ratti*."

I stood there and stared from the bottles to Teeny to the bottles.

"The bottles are filled with water at different levels," she said.

I got it immediately.

"Yeah," she said. "You got it. The calmest breeze or the wildest wind blowing across the tops of those bottles sends vibrations down into the ground. Gophers hate noise, especially sounds of the wind and shakings of the soil."

"Where'd you get that idea, Teeny? You read it somewhere? Your mom says you're always sitting at your computer. You doing research?"

"I looked at a catalogue and saw those battery units you can stick in the ground and they vibrate and—"

"And the gophers run."

"Yeah. But I'd need maybe ten of those buggers, and each one costs thirty dollars. So, I made my own, and all I do is keep the water levels in all the bottles uneven."

Eight months later, when I harvested my garlic, I'd lost about ten percent of my crop to gophers. Teeny's loss: maybe a half of one percent.

The Marriage of Mushrooms & Garlic

On my 89th birthday, the Biaggios took me to dinner at the Union Hotel in Occidental. When the three Biaggios lifted their glasses to toast me Tony said, "Crystal's got a special gift for you, Chester."

Bianca said, "It's from Transylvania."

Teeny reached under the table and brought out a folder bound with blue ribbons. She handed it to me and then came around to stand behind me as I untied the ribbons.

Inside the folder: a manuscript, typed, freshly printed.

On the first page, in the center of the page, the title: FROM TRANSYLVANIA.

I checked the last page. The number in the upper right corner: 256.

"It's a novel," Teeny said. "It's about you and me and garlic and love and marriage and happiness and raising a family and never killing anything.   Will you read it, Chester, and maybe help me make it better and maybe help me get it published? Look at page two."

I turned to page 2. There in the middle of the page:

FOR MY BUDDY AND MY BROTHER AND MY SISTER AND MY TEACHER
AND MY SAVIOR: CHESTER AARON

Teeny Biaggio

The Wild Ones
(Bolete, Chanterelle, Morel) 69

No book written by someone who has a passion for the way mushrooms are grown, cooked and collected would ever bypass the ones that are, for the most part, still wild. The next few passages are dedicated to a few of those mushrooms that have been culinary treasures in wonderful dishes for decades, and in some cases for centuries, and that arrive at the dinner table only because someone made the effort to go out and forage for them. There are many more wonderfully delicious wild mushrooms that I would love to write about, but it would be very difficult for our readers to find them. So, I decided to stick with the big three that can be accessed much more easily.

The King Bolete Mushroom

*A*KA porcini, cep, steinpilz, and by its scientific name *Boletus edulus.*
Enter the King.

This mushroom is the favorite for many old and new European dishes and greatly favored by the Italians, French and Germans. It is also a big favorite with northeastern Europeans, Poles, Czechs and Russians. They dry them, pickle them and dry-smoke them so no *Boletus* is ever wasted.

There are several varieties, and not all of them are edible, so beware and always collect with an experienced mushroom person. As they say in my part of California, always check to make sure that person has some Italian blood.

This mushroom has a relatively short shelf-life compared to other wild mushrooms and is also very susceptible to the little fungus fly that lays its eggs on the mushroom. This often results in small white maggots that don't look very appetizing. Fortunately, they are harmless, so a little extra protein won't hurt.

Many Boletus are dried, and there is a huge market for them valued in the millions of dollars. Even China and India have gotten in on the act and are shipping dried Boletus to markets in Europe and North America. It's interesting to note that this mushroom lover has never come across an Asian dish that contained

Boletus, despite the fact that edible Boletus varieties are found in Asia. I *have* seen them in the markets in northern Thailand and Laos.

Collecting the King in our region can be quite challenging, especially if you are color-blind, as I am, with a deficit in the red-green-brown range. In the long grasses, they become quite difficult to see, so I always make sure I go out with my friend Richard. He has hawk's eyes when it comes to finding Boletus, so we rarely return home empty-handed.

The desire for this mushroom prompted me to pull together a group of foodie-friends and journey to Europe, touring in two minivans. The highlight and focus was to travel to Tuscany, Italy, where we rented a small villa in a ancient hilltop village for ten days, savoring local food and drinking good local wines.

The time of the year was autumn, and it was porcini season. Fortunately for us, the weather cooperated, and the porcini were quite abundant in the surrounding hills. How fortunate for us that our timing was perfect.

Despite their fabulous flavors, it was interesting to note that the porcini found in northern California where equally as good if not perhaps a little better.

The King Bolete (Porcini) Recipe

PORCINI RISOTTO FOR TWO

1 tbsp. dried porcini course powder
6 pieces sliced dried porcini (optional but
   desirable)
pinch of sugar
1 tsp. porcini oil (optional but desirable)
2 tbsp. grated Parmigiano reggiano
4 tbsp. butter or olive oil
$3/4$ C. dry white wine
2 C. chicken stock
$3/4$ C. arborio rice

Prepare porcini stock by placing 1 tbsp. of dried porcini powder, sliced porcini and a pinch of sugar into 1 cup warm water. Let soak for 30–60 minutes. (For the well organized, covered overnight in the refrigerator is even better.)

Cooking should take approximately 20 minutes with the recommended portions. A truly *al dente* finish is expected. Bite a piece of rice to test if done, or slice a few grains in half. They should be soft going to firm with a pinprick of white in the center (al dente).

Take the sliced porcini in your hand and squeeze out the liquid. Set aside with the rice. Mix porcini stock and chicken stock together in a saucepan and heat to almost a simmer, remove from heat and set aside.

74

Melt 2 tbsp. butter or oil in a saucepan. When good and hot, add the rice and sliced porcini. For first-time risotto makers, set the clock for 20 minutes. Stir and cook for approximately 1 minute on medium-high heat.

Add the dry white wine. Stir and simmer down until almost all the liquid has gone. Add 1 cup of prepared stock. Stir and simmer down again. (The starch should be really coming out now.)

Repeat twice again using all the stock for a total of 3 times.

When the liquid is almost gone the third time, add the remaining 2 tbsp. of butter or oil and two tbsp. grated cheese. Mix briskly 1 minute and turn off the heat. Add 1 tsp. or more to taste of porcini oil to the mixture and serve immediately.

To prepare for 4 or 6, just keep doubling the ingredients and allow a little more time.

Risotto gets better with practice, and you can make slight variations according to your own taste.

Buon appetito!

The Chanterelle Mushroom

AKA golden chanterelle, pfifferling, and by its scientific name *Cantharellus cibarius*.

This beautiful golden-orange mushroom is found in several parts of the world and is generally eaten fresh, although some are also canned and a few are dried.

Depending on the geographical location it is available for a relatively long period of time, and in the United States can be collected September through February on the West Coast and June through November on the East Coast. However, like all wild mushrooms, they are totally dependent on the weather and that will always involve rain.

The chanterelle has a number of variants. For instance, the northeastern verities tend to be smaller and often more orange in color while those on the West Coast can be huge. I have found some in the coastal areas of northern California that have weighed more than three pounds each when Mother Nature is cooperating.

Regardless of size, they are all delicious, and I love them in creamy sauces or garnishing a cheesy risotto. They go well with poultry, fish and are wonderful in an omelet.

It's very difficult to go wrong with chanterelles, but when in doubt, just involve some butter and cream.

For the simplest of dishes, take a skillet, rub it with a slice of garlic, place it on the stove and melt a piece of butter until quite hot. Add a layer of thinly sliced chanterelles, cook fast and hot until a little browned, add a pinch of salt, a little cream, sizzle it for a few moments, and then pour over a slice of toast. You can do this in five minutes. Truly a little taste of heaven.

The Marriage of Mushrooms & Garlic

Chanterelle Mushroom Recipes

CHANTERELLE MUSHROOM CREPES

Serves 4

For the crepes
1 ¹/₈ C. of milk
1 C. of flour
2 eggs
2 tbsp. melted butter

For the filling
1 pound of chanterelle mushrooms (sliced, if they
   are large)
2 cloves garlic, minced
2 tsp. of butter
¹/₄ C. flour
2 C. of half & half
salt and white pepper to taste
2 tbsp. sherry (optional)

For the crepes
In a blender or food processor, combine all
ingredients until well blended. Pour the batter
into a pitcher and allow to rest for at least an
hour. The batter can also be made the night
before and refrigerated overnight.

Butter a six-inch non-stick pan. When hot and bubbly, pour ¼ cup batter into the hot pan and swirl until bottom is coated. When set, turn crepe over and allow to sit for a minute. Crepe should be a light gold color.

Remove from pan and place completed crepe on a plate. Cover with a piece of waxed paper or foil. Repeat until batter is used up, making sure there is foil or paper between each crepe. Unused crepes can be frozen for later use.

For the filling

Sauté the mushrooms and minced garlic in the butter until soft and golden. Sprinkle with the flour and stir until well coated. Add the half & half and stir until there is a thick sauce and the mixture is bubbling. Remove from heat and add the salt and pepper to taste and the sherry if desired.

Spoon a little of the mixture down the center of each of four of the crepes. Fold the crepes into a cylinder and place each on a plate seam-side down. Spoon the remaining sauce evenly over the top of the crepes. Serve immediately.

CHICKEN BREAST IN A CREAMY CHANTERELLE SAUCE

Serve with rice or creamed mashed potatoes. Serves two. For larger portions, just double the ingredients.

2 chicken breasts
8 ounces fresh chanterelle mushrooms (sliced)

1 c heavy cream
2 tbsp. white wine (I prefer marsala)
1 small garlic clove
2 tbsp. cooking oil
pinch of salt and pepper

Heat the skillet and cook garlic in oil on medium to high heat. Place the chicken breasts in the skillet, and cook until browned on both sides. Reduce the heat a little, add salt and pepper. Add the sliced chanterelle mushrooms and cook for one minute. Add the two tbsp. of wine and reduce until the liquid is almost gone. Now add the cream and gently simmer, stirring continuously until the sauce has thickened (approximately 2 minutes).

The Marriage of Mushrooms & Garlic

The Morel Mushroom

AKA black morel, yellow morel, common morel, and by its scientific name *Morchella esculenta* (black morel: *Morchella elata*).

The morel is in good company with the chanterelle and the king bolete; together they are sometimes referred to as "the big three." It is easily recognized, as it is quite different from most other mushrooms. Growing one to four inches tall, it is conical in shape, is covered with deep irregular wrinkles, and is completely hollow, including the stem.

The morel is found almost globally, in India, China, Europe, and North America. It is available both fresh and dried, but like the bolete, it has a short shelf life. As a result, the majority are dried. This enables them to be shipped long distances and stored for long periods of time, often to be sold when prices are higher.

Although I have included it in the wild category, attempts to grow it are underway and to some degree have been quite successful. In my opinion, they have quite a way to go before they can compete with the wild collected morels. Nevertheless, I wish the researchers all the best success.

During my time with Gourmet Mushrooms, Inc., we purchased wild morels from collectors mostly located in North America. We would ship them all over the place, including France's famous *rungis* market, to Switzerland, the UK, and to fine restaurants and purveyors all over North America.

My only really in-depth experience with this sometimes elusive fungus is when I received a surprise phone call from the governor's office of Montana. Officials there needed advice on what to do with all these morels that were popping up. They'd had some severe forest fires, and morels like forest fires.

What generally happens is that, a year or two after a fire, usually in conifer forests, morels often pop up in the burn areas in tremendous numbers. So much so that they have prompted the scary saying that all you needed to be a successful morel collector was a collecting bucket and a box of matches. Very scary, indeed.

When I arrived in Montana, I was taken out to the burn areas, and just like the stories I had heard, there, on the mountainsides, was the proof.

I walked to the unaffected area looking for morels and after an hour of searching found only three. Then I stepped into the area that had burned a year or two earlier, and lo and behold, the morels were popping up all over the place. A real bonanza that would last for a couple more years, decreasing each successive year.

There are so many wonderful dishes that have been created using the morel. I prefer them dried and then rehydrated. The taste tends to be more intense and, like fine wines, seems to improve with a little aging.

The bar was set very high when I was traveling in Italy with my business partner David. We stumbled on this busy little restaurant in Bologna, and I ordered a morel risotto. I was in culinary heaven. I have tried to duplicate that risotto many times but always fall short of those incredible flavors.

Please try some of these recipes, but experiment, too; and if you come up with a to-die-for risotto, please let me know.

Morel Mushroom Recipe

MORELS AND CREAM SAUCE IN PASTRY SHELLS

1 pack puff pastry shells (Pepperidge Farm)
2 ounces dried morels
1 shallot, finely chopped
2 tbsp. of unsalted butter
¹/₄ C. unsalted chicken stock
1 C. heavy cream
1 C. warm water
salt and pepper to taste

Prepare the pastry shells according to the package instruction. Re-hydrate morels in a

cup warm water soak for at least 20 minutes. Remove morels then drain the morel stock through a fine filter to remove any debris. Set aside ¹/₂ cup of the stock.

If the morels are large, cut them into halves or quarters, but if small keep them whole.

Melt one tbsp. butter into sauté pan over medium heat, add minced shallots. Sauté until they start turning translucent then add morels with a pinch of salt and pepper. Add ¹/₂ cup morel stock and ¹/₄ cup chicken stock.

Braise morels in the stock until reduced by half. Add the heavy cream and simmer until the sauce thickens. Add remaining butter, check for salt and pepper.

Place puff pastry shells on a serving plate and fill the shells with the morels and cream sauce.

Serve right away.

The Search for *Cordyceps sinensis* 83

*I*magine this.

It is May 1995. My team and I, belted into two helicopters, are flying over the Himalayas. In my team: two Japanese scientists, a complement of local Mykot guides and their equipment (aides carrying arms) and, of course, me.

When I descend from the helicopter in Nepal, I am not only a twelve-day walk from the closest suggestion of civilization I am told I am the first Caucasian ever to have appeared in this remote, wild, uninhabited region.

Why am I here?

I am searching for a rare fungus, the *Cordyceps*, a mushroom prized by the Nepalese and Chinese for its curative properties. In truth, I am searching for a rare strain of *Cordyceps*, the *Cordyceps sinensis*.

The odds for the discovery of any strain of this specific mushroom are barely fifty percent, at best. This is a well organized trip that has been two years in the planning; but Dr. Yoshi, who had been here some fifteen years earlier, had established contacts and made friends, now has to be evacuated off the mountain because of altitude sickness.

The odds are not improved by a possible attack by Communist separatist groups wanting to overthrow the government of Nepal.

It is almost impossible to describe how this single specific journey onto the Himalayan slopes and the successful search, not just for a specific mushroom but for a specific strain of that mushroom, illustrates the life I have—sometimes consciously, sometimes unconsciously—designed for myself. There are days when I am not sure whether I should refer to my existence as the life I love or the life I live.

The *Cordyceps sinensis* grows generally on the southern exposure of the mountains and at an elevation of approximately 12,000 feet. When these slopes of the high Himalayas are warmed by the spring sunshine, the surface temperature, for three or four hours each day, can reach 60° F

(15° C). It is only in the spring, and only on these slopes, that this elusive *Cordyceps* emerges from its long winter dormancy.

Our Mykot guides had told us that should we find the high elevation primrose (*Primula* sp.) in bloom, we would go on to find the *Cordyceps*. Such information proved helpful for a not necessarily scientific reason. Searching for evidence of the primrose would distract us from concentrating on the skies, a normal practice in the high Himalayas, where the sighting of evidence of incoming storms can save your life. Over the years the ferocity of such storms, catching mountaineers off-guard, has been an accomplice in many tragedies.

Observing the skies less and the terrain more led us to finding the primrose and, subsequently, just as the Mykot guides had predicted, to the *Cordyceps*.

Among all the fabulous fungi I collect and study and strive to reproduce on my farm, in my lab, I find the survival technique of the *Cordyceps sinensis* unique. The spore of the *Cordyceps* inhabits a particular caterpillar larva. Over the winter, while enduring the sub-zero temperatures of the high Himalayas, the mycelium consumes the entire larval body. Once the host is completely colonized, with the larval body mummified and only the outer shell remaining, the mushroom, ready to reproduce, sends forth its fruiting body.

Although the method by which the *Cordyceps* invades its host's body is not yet understood, my own research suggests that the spore is ingested. After ingestion, the spore begins to germinate (to grow or sprout) inside the larva's body. As it germinates, it sends its mycelium (the vegetative stage of a mushroom) through all parts of the defenseless caterpillar-host, killing it.

In the spring, the fruitbody of the *Cordyceps* emerges through the shell of its host and protrudes up through the grass, resembling a tiny three-to-four-inch worm seeking to escape its home in the soil in search of a bit of sun.

Given a density of approximately one mushroom per ten square yards in a good collection site, a forager can sometimes spend many hours, even days, before finding a single *Cordyceps*.

We did view the beautiful spring primrose that day, and verifying the predictions of the Mykots, we found and retrieved twenty-seven living specimens not just of the rare *Cordyceps* but of its particular and even rarer strain, the *Cordyceps sinensis*.

Having worked for several years in the establishment of a process for culturing the *Cordyceps sinensis*, I was prepared for this moment of discovery. Six days after rising up out of the Himalayas with my specimens, I was in my lab in Sebastopol, California. Within ten months my company—Gourmet Mushrooms, Inc.—was producing a bio-mass of *Cordyceps*.

A word about the complex process of naturalizing or cultivating. Your indulgence, please, for a moment of specialized vocabulary.

Each of the thousands of species of mushrooms in the world has a variety of active compounds, such as glycoproteins, polysaccharides, complex enzymes, alkaloids, glucans, triterpenoids,

nucleotides and many other important compounds. Many researchers believe a combination of these compounds, present to various degrees in different mushrooms, can benefit the human immune system and can aid in such functions as neuron transmission, metabolism, hormonal balance and the transport of nutrients as well as oxygen.

Compounds derived from a certain strain of the *Cordyceps* can be a powerful stimulant for macrophage activity, which strengthens the immune system's ability to fight against bacterial and viral infection. Human clinical studies in China show that *Cordyceps* is effective for treatment of high cholesterol, poor libido, arrthythmia, lung cancer, and chronic kidney failure. As a tonic that causes relaxation of the smooth muscles, *Cordyceps* is especially helpful for treating chronic cough, asthma, and other bronchial conditions. The tonic can both stimulate the endocrine system and serve as an antibacterial agent.

All the above provides me now with the opportunity to explain, briefly and clearly, what we do in our laboratory at Gourmet Mushrooms, Inc. in California.

Some distributors of mushrooms describe their product as "standardized." The term is a risky choice. Attention must always be paid to the process by which this so-called standardization occurs.

In the industry at large, some compounds such as polysaccharides and lipids are artificially used as markers for standardization. These markers may or may not truly represent the quality of the product, because every species and every strain of mushroom has many ingredients, each of which is very complex. At our laboratory, to create a "fingerprint" or reference base for comparison of each of our products, we rely on an analytical method called *capillary electrophoresis*. Repeating the same tests periodically—such as using our own tested cultures and controlling the pH, the temperature and the light—we are able to monitor consistency.

This tight control of cultivation, this monitoring of consistency, ensures minimal variations. And minimal variation assures the product of medicinal mushrooms has not just the highest but the most consistent qualities.

86 For the cultivation of our mushrooms, we use specially designed containers filled not with soil but with sterilized organic substrates such as organically cultivated grain formulations. This cultivation process was created by the late Dr. Tsuneto Yoshii, my mentor, the innovator of the use of wood-fiber substrate for mushroom cultivation. I studied and worked and collaborated with Dr. Yoshii for more than thirty years. Dr. Yoshii sincerely believed that the benefits of medicinal and culinary mushrooms should be spread throughout the world. Acting on his philosophy, he shared his unique cultivating process with Taiwan, Korea, China and myself.

Here at Gourmet Mushrooms, Inc. in our special containers, the mycelium digests the specially formulated organic substrates until it's ready to produce the *primordial* (the beginning of a fruit body), which contains much of the energy and vitality that is produced and stored in the mycelial mass. This unique growing process ensures the mushroom's freedom from environmental pollutants and toxins.

Remember: wild mushrooms grow in an extremely hostile environment, at the low end of the food chain, finding nutrition in fallen trees and decayed material, competing for life with various levels of different forms of bacteria, yeast and other fungi. Because mushrooms excrete their digestive enzymes outside of their cells, and because these excretions immobilize certain pathogens present, our cultures are able to reabsorb the digested now-uncontaminated nutrients back into their cells.

It should be no surprise that, when compared with other plant medicinals, fungi can provide exceptionally powerful immune-system support.

Miscellaneous Recipes

MIXED MUSHROOM PATE

*8 ounces mixed mushrooms varieties (Gourmet
    Mushrooms, Inc. Chef Sampler pack) chopped
    into small pieces*
1 shallot, finely minced
2 tbsp. olive oil
1 tbsp. sweet butter
1 tbsp. heavy whipping cream
¼ tsp. salt
pepper to taste
1 tbsp. sweet marsala wine (or sherry)
pinch of cinnamon

Sauté shallots in olive oil until translucent,
then add chopped mushrooms and cook for
5 minutes or until a little brown. Add marsala
wine and cook for one minute then add butter and cream.

Next add a little salt and pepper, cook for
another minute, and place mixture into a food
processor. Add a pinch of cinnamon and blend
until smooth.

Place into a suitable container and serve.

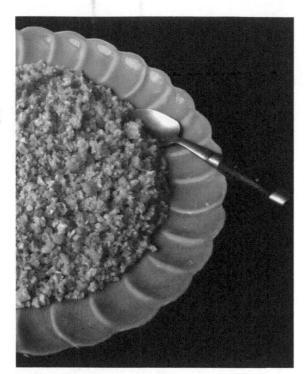

PIC'S PREPARED GARLIC

Fast and convenient. Good over salads, prepared meats or as a garnish. This is a staple in Thai kitchens.

16 oz. of fresh garlic, peeled
1 C. of vegetable oil of choice

Using a blender or food processor, mince garlic to the size of rice grains. Heat oil but do not let it get to the smoking point. Add prepared garlic and stir constantly until it turns a light brown. Remove garlic and place on a paper towel to drain.

Store garlic in an airtight container, such as a screw-cap jar.

You can use garlic oil for salad dressing or as dipping for bread, if you wish.

My Cat *Goldy*

Today is Goldy's birthday. She is six years old. She does not want a party. She wants garlic.

For the first three years of her life, Goldy ate whatever I put before her, whether it was canned food or kibble or milk. She would refuse the milk if it were cooler than room temperature.

Then in her fourth year, two years ago, her life changed.

So did mine.

Goldy is a sunlit cloud of a cat. Her long hair (if I call it fur, she scowls and hisses) is straight, uncurled, orange with a teeny hint of red. As a kitten, she was a fluffy furball.

Right up to today, she has always been so beautiful and charming that cars moving on the dirt road that cuts through my tiny farm often stop, and passengers old and young, male and female, whistle and snap fingers and croon prayers in an effort to lure the orange furball into their arms for photographs.

Goldy has never submitted.

Reigning queen of the feline world, Goldy sits in the grass at the side of the dirt road and stares up at whoever is waving their arms and hoping for photographs; and then, at the last moment, she leaps and races into the safety of the field's tall grasses and the now-30 boxes in which I grow my now-47 varieties of garlic.

When I brought Goldy home from the Humane Society six years ago, two months after her birth, she chose, for about a month, to stay in the house. Then she demanded to be wherever I might be. She was happier to join me and stay with me outside.

When I worked in the field, Goldy was there to supervise. When I was outside, repairing one or another of the boxes I use for planting my garlic, Goldy was there, enduring the noise if and when I used my chainsaw or my drill or my hammer. When I took a break to eat or drink or nap, Goldy followed me into the house to eat or drink or nap.

Until two or three weeks ago, she was extremely disciplined. Her life was a very simple ritual. Every morning, at sunrise, she leaped from my bed and rushed downstairs to wait at her

bowl. Every day, at noon, no matter my activities inside or outside, she was there at her bowl on the floor in the kitchen, waiting. Every evening, when I was setting my supper on the table, she sat at the bowl, waiting.

Whatever I served her she gratefully, happily, consumed.

Then one day, about three weeks ago, she discovered a gopher in Box 10, and she killed it and, of course, ate it. I think she considered the beast a mouse or rat.

It so happens that Box 10 contains inchelium red garlic, a softneck artichoke variety, a garlic that, for me, is hot on neither the tongue nor the palate. Its flavor, for me, is always mild.

That moment, when the gopher, which had been consuming the inchelium red, was eaten by Goldy changed her life forever. From that moment, she scorned whatever food I placed before her in her bowls. Every hour of every day (and occasionally nights) she was outside at the boxes, waiting. She still visited her water bowl in the kitchen, or the bowl in which, once a week, I served her milk (at room temperature), but she spent her days (and occasionally evenings) at Box 10 or 11, waiting for a gopher and, when catching one, eating it.

I needed no question-answer exchange to convince myself it was the garlic flavor that had changed Goldy's requirements for edible food. Occasionally suspicious of my often brilliant analyses, however, I intended this time to prove the validity of my talents.

I set out two bowls of kibble. One bowl contained the regular kibble, straight from the plastic bag. One bowl contained the regular kibble into which I had pressed and stirred one clove of a miscellaneous garlic. This miscellaneous garlic was a resident from the jar near my kitchen stove that contained dozens of unidentified and unidentifiable garlic cloves reserved for random use.

Goldy scarfed up every single kernel of the garlic-flavored kibble and raced upstairs and jumped onto my bed and fell asleep immediately.

For a week or two, Goldy ate whatever I offered in the bowls, which just happened to be infused with pressed cloves of that random, unidentifiable garlic.

Then, about a week ago, life changed again. Mine changed, too, of course.

In addition to the garlic-tainted kibble I was feeding her inside the house in her bowl, Goldy, for about three weeks, had been killing and eating an occasional anonymous gopher found in this or that box filled with this or that garlic variety. Then about a week ago, I happened to notice she was concentrating on Box 19, killing and eating only a gopher caught in or near that box. Gophers

The Marriage of Mushrooms & Garlic

caught in the open field or at one of the other 29 boxes were left to rot in the field or be scarfed up by the buzzards.

I also noticed that Goldy was no longer eating the kibble in that bowl in the kitchen.

Again my experience and my need to validate my genius benefited both of us. Box 19 (I reminded myself) contained a rare garlic I had started planting only last year: French Germinador (a hardneck purple stripe,) a garlic I had received from a beautiful young Frenchwoman I'd met at a party in Berkeley.

When, at the party, Lise Helene Trouillaud learned I was a garlic farmer who was not only growing many different varieties from several different countries but was also writing and publishing books about my experiences with garlic and garlic growers, she—Lise Helene Trouillaud—wrote her mother about me and sent her one of my books.

Her mother sent Lise Helene garlic just for me, garlic she had purchased at a farmer's market near Marsilly, in France.

My Cat *Goldy*

Lise Helene and her boyfriend delivered ten bulbs to me here in Occidental; and I, after tasting one clove (and then a second to verify my reactions to the first,) planted every clove remaining. A total of 56.

I planted almost every clove of every bulb that I harvested this year. The few cloves I ate reminded me that this was, indeed, a rare garlic. I knew that, being of such rare delicacy, this garlic might be difficult—even perhaps, impossible—to continue to grow in my soil in my weather. But try I must and would.

Goldy, the epicure, having tasted, indirectly, the unique qualities of the French Germinador garlic, now scorned every food I offered her unless the garlic I used was the French Germinador. To possess enough for the coming planting season, and to create a sacred stash for Goldy, I would have to be very, very detailed in my calculations.

The Marriage of Mushrooms & Garlic

Working for six hours, I poured into my food-processor six cups of water and one pound of peeled French Germinador cloves—two hours of labor at the sink. After pressing the buttons for chopping and then mixing and then puree-ing the mix until it was the consistency of wet sawdust, I poured the substance into one-cup containers. The container currently in use would rest in the fridge until it was empty, and the remaining containers, stuffed, would wait in the freezer for their turn to be used.

The plan is working as if it had been conceived by Einstein.

One-half tablespoon of the garlic (at room temperature) mixed into the bowl of kibble has been keeping Goldy so contented she no longer goes into the field to chase gophers.

To satisfy my continuing doubts regarding my wisdom, I tried, yesterday, pressing a different variety of garlic into the kibble. Goldy, at her bowl, turned up her wet pink nose in feline scorn. I replaced that bowl with a new bowl containing kibble mixed with my concoction, and the bowl was emptied in ten minutes.

Goldy, after licking the bowl, pasted kisses of gratitude on my face.

"It's just you, babe," Goldy sang. "It's just you I'm lookin' for, babe … "

How can I not believe that Goldy's lineage goes back not to Napoleon but to Marie Antoinette?

My Cat *Goldy*

Suggested Garlic Varieties

TASTE ACCORDING TO CHESTER

The taste of individual garlic varieties, like the taste of wine from different grapes, is widely variable due to differences in soil, climate, water, fertilizer and other growing factors. In addition, each taster imparts her/his unique chemistry to the mix.

ARMENIAN

Hardneck Rocambole

From the village of Hadrut Karabagh, Armenia, via Sylva Bagdasarian, a Berkeley art dealer who found the bulbs in her relative's field. Extremely tough and durable. Ideal for roasting. Moderately easy to peel. Taste, for me: strong, earthy. Shelf-life: 4–7 months.

BURGUNDY

Softneck Silverskin (Creole Group)

Creole Group includes ajo rojo and Creole red. Original source of this garlic unknown, possibly France/Germany. Small cloves' skins are deep burgundy in color. Garlic ignored because of size of cloves and because the cloves are hard to peel; but the taste, for me, is very rich, with a light bite that is not long-lasting. Shelf-life: 4–6 months.

INCHELIUM RED

Softneck Artichoke

Seed from David Cavagnaro at Seed Savers Exchange. Originally from Colville Indian Reservation in state of Washington. Considered by some to be the oldest garlic in North America. Used by Native Americans. In a 1990 taste test at Rodale Gardens, it was rated top softneck garlic. Taste, for me: dense but mild and lingering. Shelf-life: 5–7 months.

(ROSEWOOD)
Hardneck Rocambole

Seed from Garlicsmiths in Washington. Originally frrom Siberia. Tall, elegant plants with 4–6 beautiful elongated cloves. Grew very well the first year in bad weather. Fine garlic for roasting. Taste, for me: not too hot, rich taste remains long after. Shelf-life: 4–6 months.

LAMPANG
Unclassified

Seed from Poul Palmer, The Garlic Guy, who obtained it from Avram Drucker, where it took five years to adapt to his growing environment. Original seed collected at a roadside stand between Lampang and Lamphun south of Chaing Mai, Thailand. Taste, for Poul: very hot.

THAI PURPLE
Hardneck Turban

Seed from Filaree Farm. Originally purchased in a Bangkok market. Filaree's seed from Salt Spring Seeds via Flora Baartz. Bulb-wrappers have purple blush. 6–8 large cloves with light reddish mahogany skins. Taste, for me: light bite, not long-lasting. Shelf-life: 4–6 months.

TRANSYLVANIAN
Softneck Silverskin/Artichoke

Seed from Prof. Robin Miller (Brandeis University). She found it in a Transylvanian market in 1993. This garlic is difficult to grow and unpredictable. Bulbs range from small to moderate, although cloves have come to triple their original size. The process has taken almost ten years (after losing 98% each season). Cloves are difficult to peel. Taste, for me: mild until late in the mouth, then strong and hot. Shelf-life: 4–6 months.

ROSE DU LAUTREC
Hardneck Rocambole

From Garlic King Farms in Colorado around 1990. This is a French red from the Tarne region. Medium-to-large bulbs with purple wrappers (skins). 8–10 cloves to a bulb. Favors mild winter climates. Taste, for me: not too hot but very pungent. Shelf-life after harvest: 5–6 months.

TUSCAN RED

Softneck Artichoke

From a market in Livorno via Lisa and Butch Llewellyn, Li Hue, Hawaii. Bulbs medium in size with 10–12 long, slender cloves. Wrappers are white, clove skins are pale brown. Taste, for me: dense, with slight bite, slight heat.

UKRAINIAN BLUE

Softneck Artichoke

Seed from Dnepropetrovsk, the Ukraine. Given to me by Malea Barber (Tulsa, Oklahoma). Her friend, Jack Kovacs, on a Mission trip, purchased the garlic on a street corner from a woman who is an engineer earning extra money growing and selling garlic. Taste, for me: very aromatic and very strong but not too hot. Shelf-life: 4–6 months.

About the Authors

MALCOLM CLARK

Malcolm was born in 1942 and later educated in the United Kingdom. His life has evolved around various fields of natural science since he graduated university. He has worked and studied in several countries on several continents, including Africa, Europe, Asia, and North America.

After working in various biological laboratories, he decided to make a radical detour and emigrated to the United States. With partner David Law, he founded a specialty mushroom cultivating company in northern California called Gourmet Mushrooms Inc. and, several years later, another company in Europe named Mycology Research Laboratories in which he is still actively involved.

In the late eighties, Malcolm opened a restaurant with partner Brian Lau called Truffles in his small Northern California hometown of Sebastopol. It was an instant success and received many magazine and newspaper food column write-ups. Alas, the mushroom operation became more and more demanding, and three years after opening, they decided to sell the restaurant.

Over the years, Malcolm has been a guest speaker at various mushroom conferences in Europe, Asia and North America and has always maintained that practicing the art of science was key to his success. Now semi-retired, he divides his time between his home in beautiful Northern California wine country and his second home in Chiang-Mai, northern Thailand. In both locations, he continues to pursue his second passion, growing and breeding orchids and traveling to exotic destinations.

100

Chester Aaron was born in Butler, Pennsylvania, in 1923; he graduated from Butler High School in 1941. After working in steel mills for two years, he enlisted in the US Army, where, until the end of the war, he served as a heavy machine-gunner in a heavy weapons company of the 20th Armored Division. He participated in the liberation of the concentration camp at Dachau.

After the war, he attended UCLA for three years then earned his undergraduate degree at UC Berkeley and his masters degree at San Francisco State University.

After working for ten years as Chief X-Ray Technician at Alta Bates Hospital in Berkeley, he accepted a position as a professor in the English Department at Saint Mary's College of California. Retired from Saint Mary's, he is currently Professor Emeritus.

While at Saint Mary's, he was also a garlic farmer. For more than 35 years, he grew approximately 60 varieties of garlic from 20 different countries. He has published three books—one with *Mostly Garlic* magazine, two with Ten Speed Press—about garlic-farming. Two of those books were memoirs. One, *The Great Garlic Book* is currently published by Random House.

He has also published 20 novels (adult and young adult) and short stories in *Coast Lines*, *North American Review*, *Texas Quarterly*, and *MANOA Journal* (University of Hawaii). His books have been published in Britain, France, Germany, and The Netherlands.

He has received grants and awards from the Huntington Hartford Foundation, the Chapelbrook Foundation, the Primo Levy Foundation (University of Venice) and the National Endowment for the Arts.

Chester lives in Occidental, California.

The Marriage of Mushrooms & Garlic

SURACHET SANGSANA (PIC)

Pic was born in Bangkok, Thailand. He received his BA degree in business and practiced as an analyst and advisor for small businesses in Thailand.

After coming to the United States, he worked in restaurants owned by friends and family. There, he developed a passion for presentation of Thai cuisine that became all-engrossing. At Gourmet Mushrooms, Inc., in California, Pic was involved with all aspects of the production of their Neutraceutical mushroom facility for medicinal mushrooms.

In his so-called spare time, Pic continues offering his culinary art to both private families and coordinators of large events.

SUZANNE ADAMS

Suzanne developed an appreciation of good food from her grandmother's cooks. During the sixties, she was addicted to cooking shows, cookbooks and food magazines. She loved eating in good restaurants then duplicating the dishes at home.

A career transfer in the corporate world brought her to Northern California where, on weekends, she studied at the California Culinary Academy. On the first Christmas after she and Roger moved to their farm in Occidental, she catered a party for 70 guests. That started their catering business. She left the corporate world and catered nonstop for the next thirteen years. The business progressed by word-of-mouth only, and their phone rang off the hook. She also taught classes for ten years in Bodega Harbor that always had waiting lists of applicants.

About the Authors

During that time, Suzanne and Chester had a food column in the *Bodega Bay Navigator* called "Tongue in Cheek." Suzanne prepared meals for a few close friends, and Chester wrote the text.

The move a few years ago to Sonoma led to her being chosen as a part-time chef at a winery where she is on-call. She serves as a personal chef to the owner and his family and friends when he lives at the winery in the summer.

She continues to cook for friends and enjoys the pleasures that come from it.

ROGER ADAMS

Roger received a BS in civil engineering from the University of California-Berkeley, then practiced as a licensed professional engineer fior several firms and industries.

Following his professional career, he worked with Suzanne in their catering business while teaching computers at Santa Rosa Junior College. After meeting Chester in the early nineties, he fell in love with garlic growing. He continues to grow more than thirty varieties, most of them obtained originally from Chester. He has always been an avid photographer, especially of nature and plants, so when the opportunity came to photograph mushrooms and garlic: "I couldn't pass it up."

About the Designer

STEPHEN TIANO

Stephen developed an appreciation for the written word at a very young age, writing his very first story when he was four years old. At about the same time, he had his first experience as a foodie, tasting scungilli fra diavolo unexpectedly and, consequently, his first taste of ice-cold beer to wash down the heat.

Later, as a proofreader and copy editor, he cultivated a sense of how the written word can be best displayed on the printed page.

While working as a court clerk in New York State's Unified Court System for the past 30 years, Stephen has simultaneously made time to freelance as a book designer, page compositor, and layout artist, helping to publish approximately 100 books during the last 22 years. All the while, he indulged his love of garlic, hot peppers, and cooking in general.

Stephen lives on the East End of Long Island with his wife Nannette, also an artist working in multiple media and photography, who has learned to live with her husband's tendency to sauté a whole head of garlic with his morning eggs.

Garlic Books, Posters and Suppliers

BOOKS AND POSTERS

Garlic Kisses by Chester Aaron (Zumaya Publications, Austin, TX)

The Great Garlic Book by Chester Aaron (Random House)

Garlic Is Life by Chester Aaron (Ten Speed Press, out of print)

Growing Great Garlic by Ron Engeland (Filaree Farm)

Tomatoes Garlic Basil by Doug Oster

In Pursuit of Garlic by Liz Primeau (Grey Stone Books)

The International Garlic Cookbook (Collins Publishers, San Francisco)

The Beauty of Garlic Poster by Roger Adams (www.thebeautyofgarlic.com)

SUPPLIERS

Bobba-Mikeís Gourmet Garlic Farm (www.garlicfarm.com)

South Road Garlic Farm (www.southroadgarlicfarm.com)

The Garlic Store (www.thegarlicstore.com)

Filaree Garlic Farm (www.filareefarm.com)

Poul Palmer, The Garlic Guy (www.garlicguy.net)

www.garlicmaster.com

Bob Anderson, Gourmet Garlic Gardens (www.gourmetgarlicgardens.com)

FRESH MUSHROOMS AND MUSHROOM PRODUCTS

Gourmet Mushrooms Inc

P.O. Box 180, Sebastopol, CA 95473

Phone: 707-823-1743

www.mycopia.com

Gourmet Mushrooms, Inc. was established over thirty years ago and is the true pioneer of exotic mushroom cultivation in North America.

It is certified organic and ships nationwide.

GMPH
P.O. Box 515
Graton, CA 95444
Phone 707-829-7301
www.gmushrooms.com
Suppliers of organic mushroom growing kits, mushroom arts and crafts, books, posters, etc.

For more mushroom information contact your local mycology society for Mushroom Nutraceutical/ functional food products.

In North America contact:
Mycology Research Laboratories
MRL-USA
P.O. Box 471720
San Francisco, CA 94147-1720
Phone 888-675-8721
e-mail info@mrlusa.com
www.mycologyresearch.com

In Europe contact:
Mycology Research Laboratories
info@mycologyresearch.com

Mycology Research Laboratories was established over 12 years ago and is considered the world leader in mycological health support products, shipping to more than twenty countries.

It is a sophisticated company and is credited for supporting important clinical investigations in nutritional and medical research.

It supplies a range of mushroom products in tablets and powder form. It also produces a line of domestic pet products.

CPSIA information can be obtained at www.ICGtesting.com
Printed in the USA
BVOW10s1452261213

340154BV00001B/1/P